The British Navy

A CONCISE HISTORY

OLIVER WARNER

The British Navy

A CONCISE HISTORY

with 151 illustrations

THAMES AND HUDSON · LONDON

To ARTHUR MARDER,
historian of the Navy renewed by Lord Fisher

Frontispiece: the *Resolution*, symbol of all that is
positive in the history of the British Navy.
Commissioned in 1667, the ship fought in a number
of important actions, ranging from the Texel in
1673 to Barfleur in 1692, but was eventually lost in
a gale in 1707. Painting of 1667 by Willem van de
Velde the Younger.

Printed in Great Britain by
Jarrold and Sons Ltd, Norwich

CONTENTS

Preface   6

1   Foundations   9

2   War with the Dutch   29

3   The King over the Water   49

4   The Seven Years War   67

5   The Navy in Adversity   81

6   The Long Struggle with France   93

7   Many Inventions   123

8   The First World War   137

9   The Ultimate Trial: the Second World War   151

10   Later Events   169

Suggestions for further reading   181

List of Illustrations   185

Index   189

PREFACE

Dr Johnson, in his majestic eighteenth-century dictionary, defined 'navy' as 'an assembly of ships, commonly ships of war', and this is how the word is still used. Like most institutions, the British Navy evolved: it did not spring like Minerva fully armed from the brain of Jupiter; it grew or changed to meet new circumstances. Its special concern has been the defence of the home islands and of the territories overseas which once formed part of the Empire. Its other main purpose has been the protection of the overseas trade upon which the health and prosperity of Britain so largely depends.

The distinction between the mercantile fleet and the navy which defends it in time of war has so long been evident as to be taken for granted. Nevertheless, a specialist navy, designed for fighting alone, developed by a gradual process, since wooden ships of war could be, and often were, adapted for trade, and in some cases the converse held good. The necessity for a purely naval establishment arose largely from the fact that such a force was deployed elsewhere, notably in Spain, Holland and France. Unless the country's trade, and its chance for expansion, were to be blighted, Britain had to follow suit. In course of time, in at least certain skills and accomplishments, she herself led the way.

In the Tudor age, when the story of the Royal Navy really begins, most of the principal fighting ships belonged in a very complete sense to the sovereign. Yet the flagship at the time of the Spanish Armada, the *Ark Royal*, had been built as a private venture by Sir Walter Ralegh and had indeed been named *Ark Ralegh*. The vessel was handed over for the Queen's use and did noble service with Lord Howard of Effingham, but the *Ark Royal* is in herself evidence that at least up to the year 1588 it was possible for a private person to build a major man-of-war. In the long run, however, it became clear that only the state, acting in the name of the Crown, could afford to build, equip and maintain a fleet. It was thus that the Royal and British Navy became identical, for with the union of the English and the Scottish crowns after the accession of James I in 1603, the term 'British Navy' could be applied with exactitude to the maritime armament of the British Isles.

The aim of the present account, which from the size of the subject in all its ramifications cannot hope to be inclusive, has been to show how the Navy grew from modest beginnings and how it has served as an instrument of national policy.

The writer was appointed to the Secretariat of the Admiralty at the height of the Second World War and served in that department of state for more than six years, including the transition from full mobilization to conditions approaching those of peace. The experience fortified a lifelong interest in a great service, which time has done nothing to diminish.

The courteous help of the Ministry of Defence is gratefully acknowledged in respect of certain later events, not yet covered by authoritative surveys. The views expressed are, of course, those of the writer and not of any official body.

O.W.

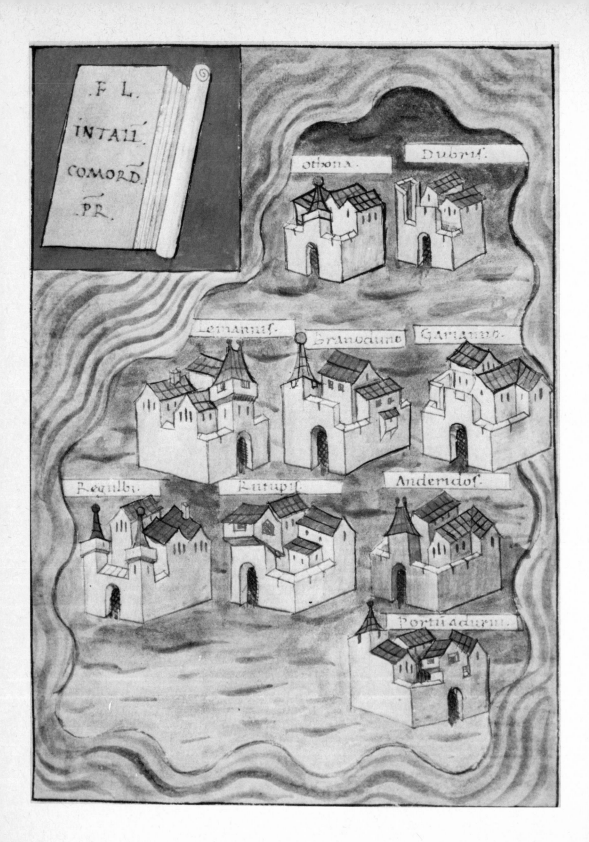

Chapter One

FOUNDATIONS

In spite of every change in the balance of world power, of national responsibilities, and of development and decline in the importance of purely maritime armaments, the identification of Britain with her Navy remains close. At one time, the Navy was part of a creed which was absorbed as a matter of course. Although this is no longer so, the idea of an island realm without a fleet invites the comparison of a mollusc without a shell.

Centuries before England was invaded and occupied successfully by William of Normandy, strategic planners had seen the need for a seaward defence, centrally controlled. This was the reason for the appointment, under the Roman empire, of an official known as the 'Count of the Saxon Shore'. He administered a series of forts or castles, extending from the Wash to Spithead; these gave protection to anchorages and housed garrisons ready to chase and round up any hostile parties which might succeed in making a landing in spite of the vigilance of such maritime forces as the Romans possessed.

As long as Roman occupation remained effective, the importance of the Count of the Saxon Shore continued. But once the legions were withdrawn, early in the fifth century, nothing permanently effective took their place. It is true that Alfred the Great, sometimes spoken of as a 'founder' of the Navy, raised and led some forces with success. But the coasts were highly vulnerable until the Normans, with possessions on both sides of the Channel and with a talent for military matters, showed themselves strong enough to protect what they held, though even they were never safe from raids and piracy.

The Norman feudal system did not include any form of permanent navy. It did, however, provide for sea service of a sort, for in the 'Domesday Book' it was noted that the town of Dover owed the King ship service for twenty ships for fifteen days in the year. The same held for Sandwich. Ships were also due from the three other towns which, together with Dover and Sandwich, became the confederation of the Cinque Ports – Hythe, Romney and Hastings.

Opposite: Romano-British forts under the control of the Count of the Saxon Shore. A late-medieval copy of a page from the fifth-century *Notitia Dignitatum.*

Winchelsea and Rye were originally 'members' of Hastings. They acquired the title of 'ancient towns' or chief ports in the fourteenth century. Various places such as Deal and Pevensey became known as 'limbs'. Here was a naval organization in embryo.

William of Normandy's larger ships, which are depicted in the Bayeux Tapestry, were Viking pattern, double-ended, clinker-built, rowed by anything between sixteen and thirty oars a side and fitted with a single mast and sail. The King's professional seamen were few. Officers and men doubled as soldiers, a process which continued all through the Middle Ages and some way beyond.

The Norman and Plantagenet Kings needed a fleet of sorts to ensure safe and regular communication with their French territories, particularly after the loss of Normandy in the reign of King John. Commerce developed extensively after the Conquest, particularly the regular wine trade with Bordeaux and the textile trade with the Low Countries, but in the Middle Ages merchants could not look to the King for much protection at sea, for the sovereign was far too occupied with his interests ashore. Traders had to be prepared to defend themselves and they were seldom above piracy. The Shipman in Chaucer's *Canterbury Tales* (*c.* 1387) occupies only twenty-two lines of description, but they tell us much. Although 'certainly he was a good felawe', the Shipman carried a dagger ready for instant use. If he fought at sea, and won, his enemies walked the plank.

Above, top to bottom: seals of Hythe, Hastings and Rye.

> *Hardy he was and wys to undertake.*
> *With many a tempest hadde his beard been shake.*
> *He knew alle the havenes, as they were,*
> *Fro Gootland to the Cape of Fynystere . . .*

By Chaucer's time, shipmen were indeed trading regularly as far as Gotland in the Baltic. There, at Visby, they were in touch with Hanseatic merchants whose routes and goods compassed most of the known world.

If defence and communication were paramount, and would always remain so, later stages in the development of the Navy may be diagnosed as being concerned with challenge and maintenance. Once

Below: Viking-type ships from the Bayeux Tapestry.

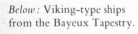

Shipman

Heere bigynneth the Shipmannes tale

A marchant whilom dwelled at Seint Denys
That ryche was / for which men helde hym wys
A wyf he hadde of excellent beautee
And compaignable and revelous was she
Which is a thyng / that causeth more dispence
Than worth is / al the chiere and reverence
That men hem doon / at festes and at daunces
Swiche salutaciouns / and contenaunces
Passen / as dooth a shadwe up on the wal
But wo is hym / that payen moot for al
The sely housbonde / algate he moste paye
He moot us clothe / and he moot us arraye
Al for his owene worship richely

Chaucer's Shipman.

a standing navy of a modest sort had been organized in the time of the early Tudors, it could be supplemented by privateers, ships in private ownership with authority from the state ('letters of marque' was a term used later for the mandate) to engage in operations against the state's enemies. The period of challenge extended from the sixteenth to the early eighteenth century, when, successively, the Spanish, the Dutch and the French possessed sources of wealth or power or both, of which Britain was prepared to fight for a share.

Once trading factories and settlements abroad had been established, and duly recognized, there followed the sometimes arduous and always protracted task of keeping what had been won. During the earlier decades of the nineteenth century, maintenance gave way to policing, in the general sense of suppression of slave-trading, surveying the sea routes and other duties which naturally devolved on the principal maritime power, as Britain had by that time become. Policing was to be followed by expansion, in a period in which the nation responded enthusiastically to Ruskin's notion of founding 'colonies as fast and far as she is able, formed of her most energetic and worthiest men, seizing every piece of fruitful waste ground she can set her foot on . . .'.

During our own century of fast change, Britain had once again to face, and ultimately to defeat, a new challenge, that from a powerful German navy. Success could not have been attained without alliances. These continue and are likely to do so for the foreseeable future, for the burst of empire has subsided and the consequent responsibilities have devolved elsewhere. The process by which these key preoccupations have been pursued must necessarily be the theme of any history of the British Navy.

In medieval times the King was never solely dependent on the Cinque Ports for ships in time of war. He possessed or commandeered others, though not always with success. For instance, when Edward III was assembling the fleet with which he fought a sanguinary battle off Sluys, on the coast of the Netherlands, in June 1340, his officers met with much difficulty, particularly on the east coast of England. So much was this so that a long list was made of ships 'which would do nothing by the King's order', some of them having 'stealthily left the Fleet, after receiving wages'. This was an early instance of deser-

The Battle of Sluys. Italian illustration to a French fourteenth-century manuscript.

tion, which later rated a column to itself in ships' muster books and was punishable by death.

The Battle of Sluys, the first of its kind on a grand scale, and important in that it made trading safer along the coasts of the Channel and the North Sea, was between some 250 ships commanded by Edward in person and about 200 French vessels in the charge of three admirals, two Norman and one Genoese, hirelings all. The slaughter was prodigious, the French losing about twenty-six thousand men, the English a sixth of that number. The ships involved were mainly small merchantmen loaded with troops. There was no tactical science to speak of. Ships grappled each other. Soldiers then boarded, under the covering fire of archers. The disparity in losses foreshadowed those of Agincourt, fought on land during the following century.

The Cinque Ports sent Edward their due quota, but their importance was steadily diminishing, so that when the next great naval mobilization took place under Henry V, by which time masted vessels had superseded galleys as the core of the fleet, their contribution was relatively small. There were various reasons for this atrophy. Among them was the steadily growing size of other ports, especially those further west like Southampton, where Henry embarked for his Agincourt campaign; ceaseless friction and jealousy between the ports themselves; and the slow action of the sea, which silted up what were once valuable havens, altering the whole aspect of the south-east coast. The Cinque Ports men were by no means above piracy and, when the country was at war, operational commanders found that they could rely more surely on other sources than the ancient, loose fraternity whose privileges seemed ever less justified. The Cinque Ports were not appropriate for a consistent maritime policy.

In one small matter, however, the Cinque Ports did truly represent the nation. Their emblem was an heraldic combination of a lion and a ship. This could have served as suitably as the white ensign to signalize the British Navy, when in due course it was regularized – the lion as the British symbol, the ship as a principal means whereby the island-kingdom is sustained.

One of the earliest exponents of the doctrine of sea power was Adam de Moleyns, Bishop of Chichester in the time of Henry V. This prelate is believed to have written a work with the title of *De Politia Conservita Maris*, usually known as 'The Libel of English Policy'. It circulated privately as early as 1436 and it was printed by Richard Hakluyt in the great collection of maritime material which he published during the following century. De Moleyns, whose career is not without irony since he met his death at the hands of sailors rioting for their pay, exhorted his countrymen to 'keepe the sea . . . shewing what profit cometh thereof, and also what worship and salvation'. His theme was that England should always remember 'the necessity of maintaining the sovereignty of the seas, whereof the peace, plenty and prosperity of the island depend'. The words have a familiar ring, for they echo those in the preamble to the Naval Discipline Act, and are not without relevance today.

De Moleyn's work was edited by Walter, first Baron Hungerford, who had fought at Agincourt, commanded a fleet assembled to raise the siege of Harfleur in 1417 and received the title of admiral, an early use of the designation. Hungerford became a Knight of the Garter and was an executor of the will of Henry V. This warrior-king was well aware of the power of disciplined ships, a fact which is vividly conveyed in the Prologue to the Third Act of Shakespeare's play about him. Henry built notable vessels, among them the very large *Grâce Dieu*, whose remains are still traceable today in the mud of the River Hamble.

It was not, however, Henry V, but the Tudors who were the true founders of a Royal Navy. Henry VII built the first dry-dock in

England. It was at Portsmouth, the year, 1497. The official responsible, Robert Brigandyn, Clerk of the King's Ships, noted the total charge as being £193 0s 6¾d, which included the dock-head and gate. The King got a bargain. The first ship to use the dock was a second *Grâce Dieu*. She was built in 1473 and was rebuilt during the following decade, when she was renamed the *Sovereign*. Henry's sense of economy, which enabled him to leave a full Treasury to his expansive son, undoubtedly extended to his ships. He also saw the wisdom of concentrating on a merchant fleet, for growth of trade was continuing side by side with exploration.

Henry VII's fleet included seven royal ships which, although designed for war, were also used for trading and were sometimes hired to merchants. Among them was the four-masted *Regent*, the largest vessel yet built in England, which dated from 1486. During the first years of his reign the young Henry VIII built another twenty-four ships, and he added to the fleet throughout his life. He emulated

The importance of the sea was recognized from an early date; gold noble of Edward III, 1360–69.

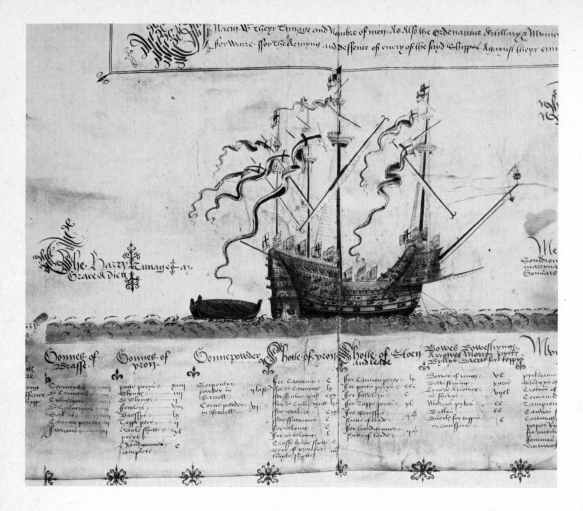

The famous *Henri Grâce à Dieu* of about 1,000 tons. In design she looked both back and forward, her fore- and aftercastles belonging to the age of hand-to-hand naval encounters, her guns a portent of the age of broadsides.

his father by building the *Henri Grâce à Dieu*, or *Great Harry*, which for her day was huge. His most important innovation was the introduction of the heavy gun, mounted on the lower deck and fired through ports or openings in the ship's side. Hitherto, naval guns had been comparatively light breech-loaders. The long era of the muzzle-loader began when it became increasingly difficult to secure the breech satisfactorily against a heavy charge of powder.

Henry had, in Sussex, the best gun-founders in Europe and he made use of them to equip his fleet in a way which would change older ideas about sea warfare. Time would be needed, and much experiment, some of it costly, before the new type of ship of war became reasonably efficient and before admirals learnt how to handle it to best advantage. It was significant that the *Mary Rose* of sixty guns, built in 1509, capsized towards the close of Henry's reign, while heeled over to tack, but with her lower ports open, drowning the Vice-Admiral, Sir George Carew, and about four hundred men. This sort of preventible disaster occasionally recurred throughout

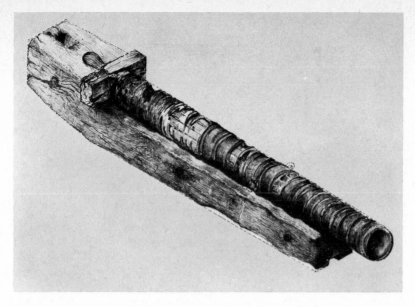

Iron breech–loading gun recovered from the wreck of the *Mary Rose*.

the era of sail, due to indiscipline, ill-management and to the inherent gap in nautical expertise between the fighting captain and the professional seamen. Carew's last recorded words, shouted across the water to his uncle, Sir Gawen Carew, were said to have been: 'I have the sort of knaves I cannot control!'

The occasion was in July 1545, when the King was opposed by a much superior French fleet, mobilized for an attempt at invasion or at least a raid in strength. Landings were made on the Isle of Wight and in Sussex, but they were defeated by the Navy and by local militia, all the forces being under the personal direction of the King.

This last campaign in which Henry took part was a highly significant confirmation of what had always been apparent: the importance he attached to the Navy. It led to Letters Patent, dated 1546, establishing a Navy Board which was to last until the time of William IV, or nearly three centuries. It was to concern itself only with the

The *Mary Rose*, whose armament included heavy guns, sank in 1545.

material side of the fleet, the strategical and tactical direction of which was to remain with the Lord Admiral – in other words, naval policy continued to be a matter for the central government. The elevated post of Lord Admiral dated from the fifteenth century, but tenure was irregular and the practical functions of the holder were not closely defined. In due course, commissioners usually took over the duties of the Lord Admiral, at such times as the sovereign did not choose to exercise the office in person.

When Henry VIII died, shortly after the issue of the Letters Patent, the enduring structure of the Navy was therefore in existence. There were ships and there was an organization to look after them. The royal fleet had, however, no regular body of officers and men, only a nucleus. The fighting men were appointed as occasion arose. The seamen were recruited, usually by force, where and when they could be found. The nucleus consisted of the 'standing officers' who acted as

ship-keepers when their charges were laid up ('in Ordinary' was the phrase which came to be used). These 'standing officers', who were the warrant officers of the future, consisted of the gunner, who looked after the armament, the boatswain, whose charge was the rigging and what pertained to the running of the ship, and the carpenter, responsible for the hull. When the time of commissioning approached, they would be joined by the master, the sailing-master responsible for navigation, the cook, and the bursar or purser, a civilian who became the ship's business manager.

The rate of pay had been fixed for the seamen in 1440 at 6s a month, but had been decreased in Henry's time by a shilling. Just before his death, it took an upward leap to 6s 8d, where it stood until 1588, when Queen Elizabeth raised it to 10s in a time of national emergency. The rate compared tolerably with that ashore, but delays in payment remained a grievance for centuries.

The English forces encamped at Portsmouth, with the French and English fleets, at the beginning of the battle in July 1545.

Elizabeth I: detail from a medal struck after the defeat of the Armada.

In 1588 the task fell to Henry's daughter, Elizabeth, of putting the Navy to the most important use conceivable, the saving of the realm from subjugation. What Philip II of Spain called 'The Enterprise of England' was designed to destroy or sweep aside the English fleet. He would then land an army on her shores, partly brought in ships from Spain and partly drawn from the forces with which the Duke of Parma was trying, without conspicuous success, to subjugate the Dutch. The campaign of the Armada was an early instance of the value of foreign help to a navy, for the success gained by Elizabeth was as much rejoiced at in Holland as in England: the Dutch even struck a celebratory medal to mark the event.

Experts consider that although Philip had an advantage in effective numbers both of ships and of men, there was not much difference in tonnage between the larger fighting units of each side. The English had kept their ascendancy in gun-founding and their shooting was better than that of their enemies. Moreover, they were in home waters, defending their country.

The Duke of Medina Sidonia, who had been given command of the Armada, kept excellent discipline among his fleet until it was scattered in an attack by fire-ships off Calais on 28 July. Afterwards, it

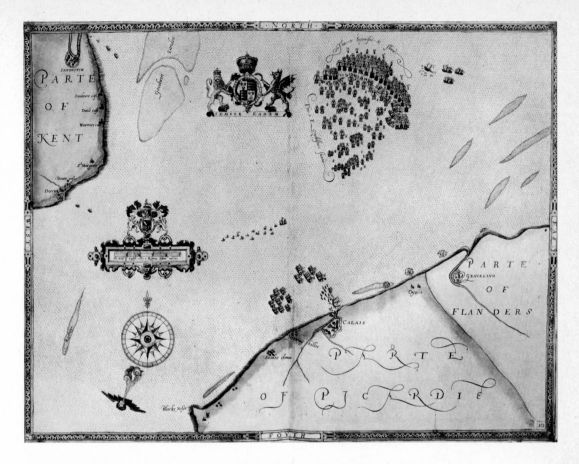

became a case of *sauve qui peut*, for the Spaniards suffered storm, harassment, sickness, and shortages of every kind, including fresh water. The captains of the ships who got their vessels back to Spain, the battered remnant of those which had set out, could consider themselves miraculously lucky.

Engagement with the Spanish Armada off Gravelines; in the foreground the fire-ships are shown being sent into Calais harbour.

The battle ranks as one of the most important in naval history. It stands first among those for which official honours were approved by the Admiralty, when in due course an authoritative list was drawn up. It did not, however, signify that Philip held himself to be finally defeated. He sent other expeditions against Elizabeth, seeking to attack her through Ireland, where she was thought to be vulnerable.

The leaders on the English side provide a roll of fame which it would be hard to equal, at least until the era of Nelson. The principal commander, Lord Howard of Effingham, represented the aristocratic hierarchy. He was a man who could expect obedience from his rank alone. His vice-admiral, Sir Francis Drake, was at the height of his powers and fame. He had not long returned from a circumnavigation of the globe, with the holds of the *Golden Hind* crammed with treasure taken from Spain in the Pacific and with a reputation as navigator and fighter which made him an exemplar of his country-

Sir Francis Drake:
Nicholas Hilliard's
miniature of 1581.

Below: the *Ark Royal*, Lord
Howard of Effingham's
Armada flagship.

men's boldest spirits. The fleet had largely been built up by Drake's kinsman, Sir John Hawkins, Treasurer of the Navy Board. Among others who sailed with Howard were Cumberland, Burrough, Frobisher and Sir James Lancaster, later famed for his voyages in the Far East.

Nicholas Hilliard miniatures of Sir Walter Ralegh (*left c.* 1585) and Lord Howard of Effingham (*right* 1605).

Sir Walter Ralegh, who might have been expected to serve afloat, was actually ashore, attending to the defences of his own West Country, but naturally he followed every phase of the sea campaign. He provided a comment, in his projected but unfinished *Historie of the World*, which occupied him when he was a prisoner in the Tower of London during the reign of Elizabeth's successor, James I. Writing of 'Sea-fights in general, and of the advantage of swift ships', Ralegh showed what a clear insight he had into the proper tactics to be employed in the particular circumstances of 1588.

> Certainely, he that will happily performe a fight at Sea, must be skilfull in making choice of Vessels to fight in: he must believe that there is more belonging to a good man of warre, upon the waters, than great daring; and must know that there is a great deale of difference between fighting loose or at large, and grappling. The Gunnes of a slow ship pierce as well, and make as great holes, as those in a swift. To clap ships together, without consideration, belongs rather to a mad man, than to a man of warre.

Of Lord Howard he writes:

> The Spaniards had an Armie aboord them; and he had none: they had more ships than he had, and of higher building and charging; so that,

had he intangled himselfe with those great and powerfull Vessels, he had greatly endangered this Kingdome of England. . . . But our Admirall knew his advantage, and held it: which had he not done, he had not been worthie to have held his head.

The honour of being considered the first systematic writer on naval tactics is usually accorded to the French Jesuit and mathematician Paul Hoste, whose folio, *L'Art des Armées Navales*, appeared in 1697. But Ralegh deserves remembrance not only for his career and for his sad death at the hands of James I, but also because he was the first Englishman who thought seriously about maritime campaigning and could apply his own experience to test what he wrote. James I himself, in his pursuit of peaceful diplomacy, did not develop the Navy, though he did launch the *Prince* in person. She was a masterpiece of Phineas Pett, who belonged to a famous dynasty of shipwrights. The vessel was named after the elder royal son, Henry, for whose edification Ralegh had composed his *Historie* and whose early death was a loss to the nation.

Ralegh's commentaries on strategy and tactics are scattered in his published works, but there also exists in the Public Record Office a series of his orders to the captains of the squadron which he took to the Orinoco in 1617 on his last expedition. He prescribed a mode of engaging an enemy with broadsides, assuming his ships to be in the windward position and in line ahead. This was the usual method of attack, when commanders could contrive it by means of very primitive signal arrangements, from Ralegh's day to the time, three centuries and more later, when lines of battleships had become obsolescent and their guns supplanted by weapons of greater range and sophistication.

Astrolabe *c.* 1588. Not all the discoveries of the Elizabethan period were achieved through advances in technology, and an ocean navigator's equipment remained relatively rudimentary until the invention of the chronometer in the eighteenth century.

Sir Richard Grenville, 1571.

Both before and after the sailing and dispersal of the Armada, Richard Hakluyt, priest, diplomatist, editor and propagandist, was engaged in putting together a tribute to the prowess of English adventurers. The first edition of his *Principal Navigations, Voyages, Traffics and Discoveries of the English Nation* appeared in 1589, the year after the campaign. A larger one followed, in three volumes, between 1598 and 1600, when there was more to include. Hakluyt was eager to encourage, by the example of selected documents drawn from many sources, the spirit of expansion which was then so active among his countrymen. It could, he argued, determine their future prosperity.

The sources of the collection were largely mercantile in origin, accounts of voyages made for the sake of trade or to examine new routes to centres of supply and exchange: but in his second edition Hakluyt included a major naval item. This was Ralegh's description of Sir Richard Grenville's fight with a Spanish fleet off the Azores in 1591, after which Drake's Armada flagship, the *Revenge*, sank during a storm. She had been engaged in an epic fight against odds, the result of calculated provocation on the part of Grenville. The narrative, which appeared within a few weeks of the battle, was stirring stuff. It became the raw material for Tennyson's poem on the same subject.

When he succeeded to the throne in 1625, Charles I found the royal ships indifferently manned and piracy shamefully rife in home waters, but he later embarked on the most ambitious project of its

Peter Pett and the
Sovereign of the Seas – the
largest fighting ship that
had ever been built in
England.

kind since the time of Henry VIII, commissioning Peter Pett to build
and decorate the *Sovereign of the Seas*. Completed in 1637, this vessel
did not belie her grandiloquent name. She was afloat for nearly half
a century and achieved many battle-honours. With her hundred guns
mounted on three decks, she was the prototype of the fleet flagship
that lasted throughout the sailing era.

Shipbuilding added to Charles's ever-present financial difficulties
and his demand for 'Ship Money' from his inland as well as from
his coastal subjects was one of the manifold causes of the Civil War,
which embittered the later years of his reign. The demand in itself
was not unreasonable. What its opponents feared was that it would
lead to corresponding pressure for 'Soldier Money'; it was also an
extra-parliamentary levy which might become permanent. The idea
of a standing army, in the control of the King or anyone else, was one

of which people had the greatest suspicion. The circumstances of the war, which led to Charles's defeat and execution, and the rule of Cromwell's major-generals which followed later, showed that their dislike was justified.

Parliament found an able servant in Robert Rich, Earl of Warwick, who for much of the struggle had charge of naval affairs. Besides a lifelong interest in the colonization of North America, Warwick had had experience of privateering. He understood the ways of seamen and the importance of good administration as well as any man of his standing.

By its early seizure and control of the principal ports and its vigilance in keeping watch on the sea routes, Parliament ensured that the King's communications overseas were at best precarious and sometimes non-existent. This was one of the more important factors which decided the issue and it was ironic that most of the best ships had been laid down by the Stuarts.

In Prince Rupert, the Royalists had a leader who, after defeat on land, seemed as much at home at sea as when leading a charge of cavalry. He did his best for a lost cause with a handful of ships, and unpaid seamen, but Parliament had a match for him in Robert Blake, an army colonel appointed 'General-at-Sea' in 1649. Blake chased Rupert away from the Mediterranean, where he had hoped to recruit,

Robert Rich, Earl of Warwick.

Robert Blake (*left*), who was first given naval command when nearly fifty, became a great fighting admiral – rival of the Royalist, Prince Rupert (*right*).

and the Prince underwent many further adventures before he was able to return to Europe and to the service of his cousin, the exiled Charles II.

One small incident in the Rupert–Blake duel is worth recalling since it was the first of a kind which, a long way into the future, was to recur often in the annals of war. In April 1650 Rupert was in the Tagus, seeking supplies from a supposedly friendly government, where he was closely watched by Blake. Determined that, if he could not damage his opponents in the open sea, he would do so by subterfuge, the Prince sent a boat loaded with fruit and other local provisions to sell to the Parliamentary crews. Two Negroes, and an English seaman disguised as a Portuguese, brought over a cask of olive oil, and a bargain was struck. But when hoisting the cargo aboard, the Englishman, sweating at the task, swore in his own language and was promptly seized. Their suspicions aroused, the Parliamentarians examined the cask with great care. Contained within it was 'a bomb-shell in a double-headed barrel, with a lock in the bowels to give fire to a quick-match'. It could also be set off by a spring, 'to be pulled by the boatman, so that it would take fire and blow up the ship'.

The seaman had been promised £100 to plant it, and the device had all the mechanical ingenuity for which the Prince was famous. It was the precursor of a long succession of increasingly ingenious lethal devices which were in time to complicate naval warfare. It was also something of a freak, a little like the conflict itself, for it was the only event of its kind in which Britain has ever been implicated.

Chapter Two

WAR WITH THE DUTCH

The Civil War within the British Isles had scarcely reached its closing stages when serious trouble developed with the Dutch. Once freed of the Spanish yoke (a fact which was formally recognized by the Treaty of Münster in 1648), the Dutch had increased their power at such a pace and with such effect that, throughout the reigns of the first two Stuarts, it had been viewed with growing concern. Two vigorous Protestant nations, whose aim it had been to curb the power of Spain and who should, from the nature of things, have stayed friends, diverged for many reasons. Their interests clashed in every part of the world where expansion seemed likely to be profitable. They were also rivals in the carrying trade; as a contemporary sea-captain put it: 'the trade of the world is too little for us two, therefore one must down'. They were united only against Spain, particularly in the West Indies: there both Dutch and English had begun to settle and in 1628 Piet Heyn had gained a spectacular success when he captured an entire treasure fleet near Havana, returning to Holland a national hero.

The first of three maritime wars with the Dutch broke out in 1652, at a time when Blake was beginning to master the art of managing a fleet. One of the main causes was a claim by the Commonwealth government, later headed by Oliver Cromwell as 'Lord Protector', to the right of searching for contraband in time of war. Cromwell also revived a claim, regarded as derisory by foreign powers, to a salute in Channel waters – and decided to enforce it. The previous year a Navigation Act, designed to benefit the country's merchant fleet, had become law. This ordained that goods were to be imported either in English ships or in those of the country which produced them. There was also fear in London that the Dutch, taking advantage of Danish weakness, might appropriate the Sound Dues which were exacted at Elsinore, the fortress guarding the main entrance to the Baltic. England was sensitive to anything which might interfere with her traffic with the Baltic countries, from which she got timber and naval stores. Owing to the huge inroads made in her oak forests, she was already experiencing a timber problem, and this was to grow ever more acute.

The question of contraband, which was thorny for centuries – as was the prevention of smuggling, which fell largely upon the Navy – had already arisen at the time when Philip II was amassing supplies for his Armada. He made use of the Hanse organization, particularly the cities of Lübeck and Hamburg, to acquire much of what he needed. After the Armada had been defeated, a number of Hanse ships in Spanish and Portuguese harbours, which had made their way to Iberia north-about to avoid interception in the Channel, were seized. The excuse was that the merchants of the cities concerned were 'arming and furnishing the known enemy of the Queen'.

The Dutch war began with a brush between Blake and Marten Tromp off Dover, when the Dutch refused to lower their topsails by way of salute. There followed battles off the Kentish Knock, at the mouth of the Thames, and off Dungeness, where Blake was worsted by a most skilful opponent.

In February 1653 the two admirals met again in a protracted fight which began off Portland. Blake got the better of the encounter, but Tromp conducted a fighting retreat all the way to the Texel. His object was to safeguard a valuable convoy of merchantmen, mainly from the East Indies, which he was at sea to protect. In this battle, Blake's fellow admirals were Richard Deane, an expert in artillery, and George Monck, a student of war by land and sea who was to pro-

The action off Portland, 18–20 February 1653.

vide a link between the Navy of the Commonwealth and that of a later time.

Monck was responsible for the successful conduct of the fleet at the Battle of the Gabbard, in June 1653, for Deane was killed by a chain-shot, drenching Monck with blood. Monck threw his cloak over the body and quietly ordered it to be taken below, in case the crew should be discouraged.

Off Scheveningen, during the following month, Monck got the better of Tromp in the course of a very severe action. Tromp himself was mortally wounded early in the fight. 'I have finished my course', he said as he lay dying: 'Have good courage.' Cornelis Evertsen kept Tromp's flag flying for the rest of the day in exactly the same spirit that Monck had shown when Deane had fallen. It was sad that such valour did not lead to a happier conclusion, for although the war ended in England's favour and led to her flag being respected through-out Europe, it settled nothing. The Dutch were unlikely to accept second place as carriers, and their race of notable admirals certainly did not end with the death of the elder Tromp.

An action off Leghorn, 12 March 1653, one of a series in the First Dutch War, many of which were indecisive.

George Monck, later 1st
Duke of Albemarle, who
won the victory at the
Battle of the Gabbard
(*right*) in June 1653.

The Battle of
Scheveningen,
31 July 1653.

When the Dutch war finished, Cromwell found himself in a position of strength. Ready to his hand was a fleet of 160 ships of all sizes, with commanders experienced in campaigning. Expansionist in his outlook, like the most eager of the Elizabethans, he decided to send Blake to the Mediterranean, where pirate squadrons from Turkey and the Barbary Coast impeded trade with the Levant, which was almost as important to England as that with the Baltic.

Blake won a significant success in April 1655 at Porto Farina on the coast of Tunisia. Then, after Cromwell had gone to war with Spain, he blockaded Cadiz, as in after years so many successors were to do. His final action was in the spring of 1657 at Santa Cruz, Teneriffe, where he attacked and destroyed a West India fleet. He died, worn out with exertion, on the homeward voyage.

Blake had made himself a professional sea officer so well equipped that he had no superior in his own generation. He has had few equals since. Clarendon, a political opponent, paid tribute to him in his panoramic *History of the Rebellion*:

> He was the first man that declined the old track, and made it manifest that the science [of controlling fleets] might be obtained in less time than was imagined; and despised those rules which had been long in practice, to keep his ship and his men out of danger; which had been held in former times a point of great ability and circumspection; as if the principal art requisite in the captain of a ship had been to be sure to come home safe again.
>
> He was the first man who brought the ships to contemn [contend with] castles on shore, which had been thought ever very formidable, and were discovered by him to make a noise only, and to fright those who could rarely be hurt by them.
>
> He was the first that infused that perfection of courage into the seamen, by making them see by experience, what mighty things they could do, if they were resolved; and taught them to fight in fire as well as upon water: and though he hath been very well imitated and followed, he was the first that gave the example of that kind of naval courage and bold and resolute achievements.

In one most important respect Blake was lucky. In Oliver Cromwell he had, as the director of strategy, a man who was himself a master of land warfare and who knew how necessary it was to leave all but the broadest decisions to the man on the spot. Tromp, on the other hand, who had to deal with five separate Dutch admiralties, was once moved to complain: 'all my trouble arises from this, that after I have contributed all that is in me to the service of the country, I may be molested on my return home with subtle questions'. Cromwell could say to Blake, 'you must handle the reins as you shall find your opportunity, and the ability of the fleet to be'. It was the injunction of a practical leader.

Cromwell, however, only stumbled to success in the West Indies. Thither in 1655 he sent William Penn, father of the founder of Pennsylvania, and General Robert Venables, with a force ill-equipped for the task it was supposed to carry out. The intention was to seize Hispaniola, the modern Haiti, which included one of the more important Spanish settlements. Penn and Venables were driven away, but rather than do nothing they landed in Jamaica, which they managed to retain. Cromwell was so angry with his commanders that he clapped them into the Tower when they returned. Later he concluded that they had done their best and released them. In fact, they had laid the foundation of future English power in the Caribbean. Jamaica proved of very high value.

In effect, Cromwell was continuing that policy of challenge which had been begun so notably during the era of Elizabeth I. As at that time, Spain was the victim, but whereas under her régime and that of the earlier Stuarts only lodgments had been made in Spanish territory, in Jamaica Cromwell had seized a base, and a potential source of wealth, of enormous importance. Port Royal, which became the principal haven, would be familiar to generations of sea officers and would be a target for the French when, in the following century, they struggled for a stronger position in the area of the West Indies and North America.

One more benefit the Navy owed to Cromwell. In January 1653 he authorized an increase in the monthly rate of pay for able seamen to 24s, with corresponding increases for ordinary seamen, grommets (who were youths apprenticed to the sea) and boys, who were to get 9s 6d. The good news was announced at seaports to the sound of trumpets. But it was one thing to authorize increases and quite another to implement them. The sailors were soon in arrears and four hundred of them burst upon Whitehall the same year as the award. One of them actually levelled a musket at Cromwell. Soldiers had to be called in to quell the disturbance, which was of a kind which had been sadly familiar at least since the time of Adam de Moleyns and doubtless long before him.

Altogether, apart from pay, Cromwell and his naval advisers had made use to great advantage of the work of their predecessors, including Elizabeth's legacy of superior gunnery and the advances of the time of Charles I towards better ship design. Moreover, it was during his régime that the emergence of a clearer spirit of professionalism began to be apparent in the Navy.

Monck, who had been a Royalist in his earlier years, changing sides after the death of Charles I, returned home to govern Scotland after his sea service against the Dutch. On Cromwell's demise, it was Monck's influence with the army which ensured that the restoration of the Stuarts was peaceful. He was at Dover in May 1660 to welcome Charles II, who created him Duke of Albemarle. It was not many years before he was called upon to resume his place at the head of an operational fleet.

Peace with Holland did not last long, for in no essentials had the commercial and colonial rivalry between the two countries been altered. By 1665 they were at war again. An early success was won by the Duke of York, later James II, who defeated Obdam off

Lowestoft and destroyed the Dutch flagship, though through a sad misunderstanding the Dutch were allowed to retreat in good order. James was a stout-hearted admiral, but his brother Charles, who had no legitimate children, did not think it right that the heir to the throne should continue to risk his life at sea. For the second season's campaign, command was given jointly to Rupert and Monck, the Prince being not unhappy to extend his experience at sea, particularly with well-found ships.

The French were in alliance with the Dutch and the English authorities made the mistake of dividing the fleet. Monck was left to face de Ruyter, the greatest of all Dutch admirals, seconded by the younger Tromp, who inherited the bravery though not the tactical ability of his father. Rupert was sent off on an alarm, which proved to be groundless, that a French force had sailed in support of the Dutch. In point of fact, England had little to fear from France at sea for some time to come.

Monck was one of those uncommon leaders whose boldness seems to have increased with age. Although he was nearer sixty than fifty at the time battle was joined on 1 June 1666, he decided that attack was the best policy, despite great inferiority in numbers. At first he got much the better of Tromp, who was in the Dutch van, but later the English lost a flagship, the *Swiftsure*, while another, the *Henry*, nearly suffered the same fate.

During the course of the first day of what was to become known as the 'Four Days' Battle', Monck was forced back by the sheer numbers which de Ruyter had with him. In the hours of darkness, Monck held a council of war with his principal officers on board the *Royal Charles*. The Admiral made known his resolve to fight on with the forty-four ships which were still in a condition to do so, despite the fact that they would be faced with almost twice their own numbers.

On the second day, Monck did well. He found that Tromp's squadron had become separated from the rest of the Dutch fleet and he attacked it with such vigour that Tromp had to shift his flag. But towards evening, de Ruyter was reinforced by sixteen fresh ships from Holland and Monck knew that further retreat was the only course open to him if he was to avoid annihilation. He sent his most damaged ships home, the rest forming a protective screen. The move was successful, though there was one tragedy. The *Royal Prince*, Phineas Pett's veteran three-decker, ran on to the Galloper Sand. She was surrounded and set on fire, Sir George Ayscue and his surviving men being made prisoner. He was the only English flag-officer to be captured during the course of the wars with Holland.

There was one stage when the *Royal Charles* herself took the ground. Rather than risk capture, Monck intended to blow the ship up, as Grenville would have liked to do with the *Revenge* when he fought the Spaniards. A young man on Monck's staff as a volunteer, John Sheffield, reported that he 'spied the Admiral charging a little pistol and putting it in his pocket', saying to those near him that he would

Opposite: James, Duke of York and brother of Charles II, was painted by Henri Gascar as Lord High Admiral. He resigned after the Test Act of 1673 precluded Roman Catholics from office.

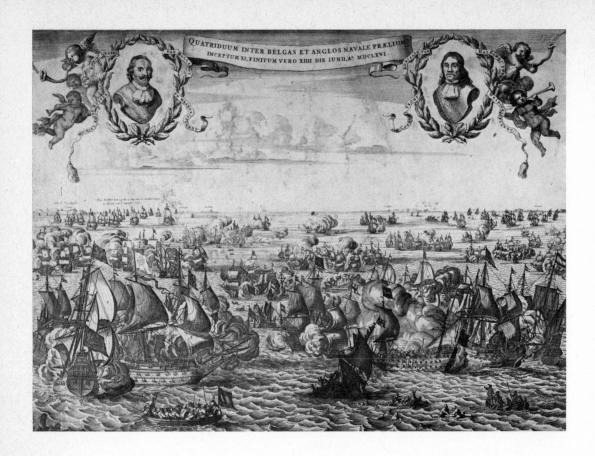

QUATRIDUUM INTER BELGAS ET ANGLOS NAVALE PRÆLIUM INCEPTUM XI, FINITUM VERO XIIII DIE IUNII, A° MDCLXVI.

The 'Four Days' Battle'. *Above:* the Dutch admirals de Ruyter (*left*) and Tromp are seen in a Dutch engraving of the action. *Opposite above:* the surrender of the *Royal Prince* to the Dutch. *Opposite below:* the *Royal Charles* burning.

never be taken. 'And', added Sheffield, 'Mr Savill and I, in a laughing way, most mutinously resolved to throw him overboard in case we should ever catch him going down to the powder room.'

The *Royal Charles* was somehow got off and soon another fleet was sighted. Was it Rupert – or the French? The Prince had in fact heard the sound of distant firing and knew how hard Monck was likely to be pressed; as there was no sign of the French, he made haste to go to the help of his fellow commander. He could not hope to reverse the unfavourable course of the action, but for the final day he was where he would have wished to be, in the thick of things.

Five times during the last phase of this most protracted encounter English and Dutch engaged in close action. Rupert's flagship, the *Royal James*, lost her mizzen yard and by evening the *Royal Charles* was so knocked about, specially aloft, that neither admiral could work his ship to advantage, or lead the fleet. But de Ruyter had also had enough. 'In the night', wrote an observer on Monck's ship, 'we mended our rigging, but the squadron having spent almost all their powder and shot, it was impossible to engage again. The Dutch left us in the night, being as unfit to fight as we, and their loss doubtless as great as ours.'

Sir Peter Lely's painting of Sir Christopher Myngs, 1666.

It was thus through exhaustion that this extraordinary battle ended, with great damage to both sides, though greater to the English, who had one flag-officer killed in action, another taken prisoner and a third, the gallant Sir Christopher Myngs – a captain in Cromwell's maritime war and still a young man – mortally wounded. Myngs had been leading the English van when he was shot in the throat. He remained on deck staunching the wound with his fingers until a second wound forced him below.

Myngs was the sort of man, not common in any armed service, who aroused extreme devotion among the rank and file of those he commanded. This was touchingly shown when his body was brought home for burial. Pepys, who was there in an Admiralty coach, records that:

> About a dozen able, lusty proper men came to the coach-side with tears in their eyes and one of them . . . spoke for the rest. . . . 'We are here a dozen of us that have long known and loved and served our dead commander . . . and have now done the last office of laying him in the ground. We would be glad we had any other to offer after him, and in revenge of him. All we have is our lives; if you will please to get His Royal Highness to give us a fire-ship among us all, here are a dozen of us, out of all which choose you one to be commander, and the rest of us, whoever his is, will serve him; and if possible do that which shall show our memory of the dead commander, and our revenge!'

Pepys commented that the offer was 'one of the most romantique that I ever heard, and could not have been believed, but that I did see it'.

It had been a costly victory for de Ruyter and he was left in no doubt as to the skill and stubbornness of the English admirals. Although Monck and Rupert lost five thousand killed, three thousand prisoners and seventeen ships, eight sunk or burnt and nine in Dutch hands, they were ready for sea again within seven weeks. On 25 July 1666, St James's Day, off Orfordness, they had their revenge, causing de Ruyter the loss of two ships to one of their own and putting him to flight. The victory was followed up smartly by Sir Robert Holmes, who destroyed 150 merchantmen in the Vlie, and burnt the store-houses of Brandaris.

This was the last cheering piece of news that England had for some time. In what Dryden called the 'Annus Mirabilis', 1666, events were mostly dire. There had been an appalling visitation of the Plague; then, in September, occurred the Great Fire of London, which destroyed most of the medieval City. The King, pressed for money and thinking that peace with Holland and France was nearer than it was, took a calculated risk and laid up the fleet. The result was a humiliation and a disaster rarely experienced by any maritime nation. In June 1667 de Ruyter blockaded the mouth of the Thames and the Medway, held London to ransom, harried such defences as had been provided and carried off the *Royal Charles*, together with other prizes, to Holland. The escutcheon of this fine ship is a treasure of the Rijksmuseum.

The escutcheon of the *Royal Charles*: a prize from one of the few successful sea-attacks made on the British Isles.

The Earl of Sandwich: Sir
Peter Lely's painting of
1666.

There were, alas, English seamen serving with the Dutch crews.
Many of them had gone over to the enemy because the pay tickets
with which they had been issued were not honoured and their
families were likely to starve. Some of them are said to have shouted
across the water: 'We did fight for tickets heretofore. Now we fight
for dollars'.

In such circumstances, Charles was lucky to make even a tolerable
peace treaty. The countries retained the conquests they had made from
each other overseas. It was thus that, in the Far East, the Dutch got
Surinam, while in North America the name of New Amsterdam was
changed to New York.

The peace proved to be only a truce, for a third war with Holland
began in 1672. It differed markedly from those of earlier years in that
it was never popular. The Dutch were defending themselves from
the forces of Louis XIV, who had designs on the Netherlands and
who had seized the enclave principality of Orange from the Dutch
house of that name, thus making at least one implacable enemy.
Dutchmen faced their giant foe in the same spirit with which, in
earlier days, they had defied Philip of Spain. Towards that attitude
the average Englishman could hardly fail to have sympathy. But for
once, French and British squadrons were ranged on the same side at

sea, an unusual event which was not to be repeated until the nineteenth century. Charles and Louis, as the architects of their own foreign policy, had come to a personal agreement.

The campaign began with a success for the English fleet at Sole Bay, when the Duke of York reappeared briefly in command, but there was also a sad loss. Lord Sandwich and his flagship the *Royal James* were destroyed in an attack by fire-ships. Sandwich's body was picked up from the sea later, many miles from the scene of the action. The Governor of Harwich reported it as 'floating upon the water, known by the George and Star' which Sandwich wore on his coat as a member of the Order of the Garter. The Admiral, added the Governor, had 'in his pocket three rings, one a white sapphire with his Crest and Garter, and the most glorious blue sapphire that I ever saw in my life.'

Lord Sandwich was given a state funeral. This was appropriate since it was he who had commanded the fleet which had brought Charles II back from exile in 1660. Among the Admiral's retinue had been Samuel Pepys. Sandwich obtained a place for him in the Navy Office and until his retirement in 1688 as the result of the flight of James II, who had become his patron, Pepys made everything which concerned the Navy his particular business. In time he came to know more about sea affairs than anyone living, not excepting the royal

The burning of the *Royal James* at Sole Bay, 28 May 1672.

brethren, Charles and James, who allowed few details to escape them concerning the fleet.

Dryden might write, with a tincture of truth:

Our careful Monarch stands in Person by,
His new-cast Cannon's firmness to explore:
The strength of big-corn'd Powder loves to try,
And Ball and Cartridge sorts for every bore.

Pepys knew to a penny the cost of naval supplies, where they came from, and into whose pocket went any profit that might be left when the 'careful Monarch' (who was never as careful as all that) eventually found the means to pay for what he had ordered.

The revelations of his diary, which is never more valuable than in such incidents as followed the death of Myngs, make Pepys better known, as a character, than anyone of his era. He also left a mass of material on naval affairs which remains invaluable and covers an astonishingly wide field. Pepys recorded the appointments and

Among Pepys's many services to the Navy were his efforts to make the best use of the finances available.

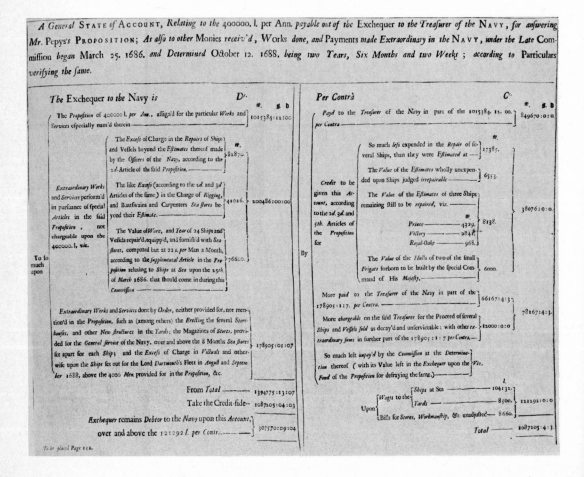

At the Restoration Pepys obtained the Navy Board post of Clerk of the Acts through his cousin Edward Montague, later Earl of Sandwich.

seniority of all the flag-officers and captains of his age and although the Admiralty did not issue an official Navy List until the reign of George I, our knowledge is close enough to apprehend in some detail the Navy which fought the wars with the Dutch.

Pepys's influence on the service, his orderly methods of administration, his pleasure that there should be a practical examination for the rank of lieutenant, thus making it more difficult for incompetents with influence behind them to achieve command, helped to make the Navy professional in the fullest sense of the word.

To Pepys's day belongs the first naval club. This was established in 1674, the members being admirals and captains, most of them eligible for the half-pay when unemployed which had recently been introduced for a few senior officers. It was a forerunner of what is now the 'Royal Navy Club of 1765 and 1785', which is itself the result of the amalgamation of two separate bodies. The members are still executive officers, mainly of high rank. Informal as the early club meetings were, since they took place over dinner, they became regular, both in peace and war. Those who forgathered were men who had commanded major ships of war on active service. They included Sir John Kempthorne, Sir Robert Holmes, Sir William Jennens and Sir William Berry, who had held posts under Prince Rupert.

For the Prince himself, the Dutch war, which occupied the best of his energies in the years 1672–74, was sad. Monck, his old comrade-in-arms, was dead and Sandwich had not long survived him. James, Duke of York, was soon excluded by the Test Act, which required those holding office to take the Sacrament according to the Anglican rite. As for the French admirals with whom he was supposed to co-ordinate his efforts, they were half-hearted allies, to use no harsher description. D'Estrée, the French commander, did so little to help Rupert that his Vice-Admiral, M. de Martell, provided an account of

an engagement which might serve as the prototype of a thousand complaints of want of support – complaints that have reverberated throughout the course of naval history and which are certainly not confined to any one nation.

> His Highness Prince Rupert seeing us come up with faire wind, gave us the Signall to beare into his wake; Monsr. de Martell laid his Sayles to the Masts, expecting that Monsr. d'Estrée would advance with his whole Squadron and fall all together with this faire wind upon the Body of the Enemy, and send his Fire Ships among them; but instead of that he kept the wind and contented himself to give his Ships leave to shoote at more than Cannon shot and half distance from the Enemy.
> Monsr. de Martell saw very well how shamefull this was; but having received an expresse order to attempt nothing without the particular Orders of Monsr. d'Estrée, and besides having been soe ill attended that morning by the Ships of his Division that he could have noe assurance they would follow him, he shrugged up his Shoulders and onely forbid any shooting from his Ships, and this hath been all that was acted that day in relation to us.

This represents an exceptionally fair account of how badly supported Rupert was, in the last considerable action of the war, which took place off the Texel in August 1673. The French writer spoke with

Fire-ships among the fleet at the Battle of the Texel, 1673.

admiration of the 'incomparable resolution' of the English, who were once more face to face with de Ruyter and Tromp. He lamented the loss of Sir Edward Spragge, who was drowned in a pinnace while transferring his flag from a damaged ship to a fresher one.

By the Treaty of Westminster, which ended the war the following year, Holland acknowledged the supremacy of England on the sea north of Cape Finisterre, agreed to an indemnity and that disputes which occurred between the Dutch and English East India Companies should be settled by arbitration.

In the same year that peace was made, the Royal Observatory was established at Greenwich. Shortly afterwards, Captain Greenville Collins was ordered by the Admiralty to survey the seas surrounding the home islands. His work superseded that of the Dutch, who were at one time the best cartographers in Europe. Collins's work appeared in 1693 under the title of *Britain's Coasting Pilot*. It was the result of surveys made between 1681 and 1688 and was the first considerable English marine atlas. It foreshadowed the later fame of the Admiralty charts, which in time covered the seas of the world.

One serious matter remained unresolved at the end of the Dutch wars and, indeed, for nearly two centuries. This was the method of recruitment of seamen for naval service. Volunteers supplied only a

Greenwich Observatory, *c.* 1680, overlooking the Thames. The Fellows of the Royal Society had persuaded Charles II of the need for the Observatory, and the monarch himself chose the site.

modest proportion, so unpopular was the Navy with those who sailed in merchantmen, and so harsh the discipline. Resort was necessary to the press gang, whose business was to conscript by force. The methods employed were brutal and led to great hardship. This was perhaps inevitable when, for example, out of a total population of less than six million, some forty-two thousand able-bodied men had to be found to man the 173 ships in commission in 1688, a year of crisis both at sea and ashore.

The upshot of affairs at that date was that James II fled the country. What was known to some as the 'Glorious Revolution' led to the eclipse of Pepys. He had become, successively, Secretary of the Admiralty, Master of Trinity House and President of the Royal Society. He had also attended James's coronation as a Baron of the Cinque Ports. The diary, which is known so well, concerns only a fragment of his life. Years before it was deciphered, when even his official work was known to few, Lord Barham, who held office as First Lord of the Admiralty during the campaign of Trafalgar and was himself a notable administrator, wrote of Pepys as 'a man of extraordinary knowledge in all that related to the business of the Naval Department, of great talents, and the most indefatigable industry'. The Navy as known to later generations was not the creation of any one man, but to Pepys may be given the credit of a devotion to its concerns which has never been exceeded. During his term of office in the largest spending department of state, he had seen the Navy established as a powerful instrument through which national policy could be implemented.

Chapter Three

THE KING OVER THE WATER

The accession of William III marked the real beginning of a new direction in British foreign policy: the inauguration of a struggle with France which lasted for more than a century. In a succession of wars, the Navy was both to support attempts to control French power on the Continent and to fulfil the crucial role in the world-wide battle for trade and empire.

James II in exile became, for confirmed Jacobites, the 'King over the Water', partly in allusion to his former naval prowess. As the years went by, they toasted him, his melancholy son and his more romantic grandson, Prince Charles Edward Stuart, with ever-diminishing optimism. But Louis XIV, William III's implacable foe, declared himself James's ally and William had to fight hard and long to keep what he had gained. James mounted a campaign in Ireland serious enough to alarm London.

William's admirals, Edward Russell, Earl of Orford ('his face a map of jolly ignorance', as a lampoonist wrote), and Arthur Herbert, Earl of Torrington, a one-eyed debauchee much disliked by Pepys, were not great men, though they were the best the King could find to carry out his strategy. They were handicapped by an even more acute shortage of money than usual. On 1 May 1689, when Torrington engaged the French at Bantry Bay, which was the focal point of communications serving James's Irish troops, he met with a rebuff, though for political reasons the encounter was hailed as a victory.

Matters improved when Londonderry was relieved, largely by naval efforts, and when in 1690 William crossed to Ireland in person and defeated his father-in-law at the Battle of the Boyne, the worst crisis had passed. Louis made strenuous efforts by sea to reverse the trend of events. He had one limited success, off Beachy Head on 30 June 1690, but a maritime campaign which followed two years later left no doubt that the Protestant succession was established and England in no immediate danger of invasion.

The clash of Torrington and the French Admiral Tourville off Beachy Head was the best opportunity the French ever had of a

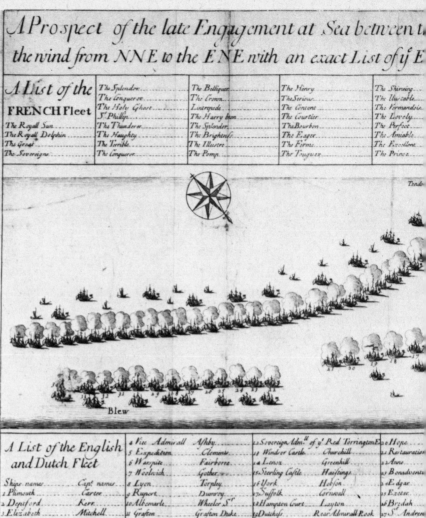

A Prospect of the late Engagement at Sea between t...

the wind from NNE to the ENE with an exact List of y̆ E...

A List of the FRENCH Fleet				
	The Splendor	The Belliquer	The Henry	The Shining
	The Conqueror	The Crown	The Serious	The Unstable
	The Holy Ghost	Intrepide	The Content	The Vermandois
The Royall Sun	St Phillip	The Harry bon	The Courtier	The Lovely
The Royall Delphin	The Thunderer	The Splendor	The Bourbon	The Perfect
The Great	The Haughty	The Brightness	The Eager	The Amiable
The Sovereigne	The Terrible	The Illustre	The Firme	The Excellent
	The Conqueror	The Pomp	The Tonguer	The Prince

Blew

A List of the English and Dutch Fleet						
	4 Vice Admirall	Ashby	12 Sovereign Adm.ll of y̆ Red Torrington	Churchill	20 Hope	
	5 Expedition	Clements	13 Windsor Castle		21 Restauration	
	6 Warspite	Fairborne	14 Lenox	Greenhill	22 Anne	
	7 Woolwich	Gother	15 Sterling Castle	Hastings	23 Bonaventure	
Ships names	Capt names	8 Lyon	Torpley	16 York	Hobson	24 Edgar
1 Plimouth	Carter	9 Rupert	Dunrvy	17 Suffolk	Cornwall	25 Essex
2 Deptford	Kerr	10 Albemarle	Wheeler Sr	18 Hampton Court	Layton	26 Brydah
3 Elezabeth	Mitchell	11 Grafton	Grafton Duke	19 Dutchss	Rear Admirall Rook	27 St Andrew

'A Prospect of the late Engagement at Sea between the English and the French fleets . . .': Beachy Head, 30 June 1690.

resounding naval victory. They had fine ships, the result of the efforts of a great Minister of Marine, Jean-Baptiste Colbert. Torrington was in greatly inferior force, for part of the English fleet was away in the Mediterranean and part was escorting William to Ireland. A Dutch squadron was present, the total of Anglo-Dutch ships being fifty-five, against which Tourville could oppose eighty.

Torrington would have liked to retreat in orderly fashion towards the Thames, to protect the capital from the penalties it had suffered a generation earlier at the hands of de Ruyter. In his own words, which became famous as expressing a permanent principle: 'Most men were in fear that the French would invade, but I was of another opinion, for I always said that whilst we had a *fleet in being* they would not make the attempt.' By no means as thick-headed as his enemies liked to make out, Torrington had a shrewd idea of French limitations and

The Proud	The Courage	The Fleron	The Vigilant	The Capable	The Positive
The Fierce	The Apollon	The St Lewis	The Wife	The Trusty	The Fawon
The Morgaue	The Diamond	The Prudent	The Hector	The Lions	The Count
The Strong	The St Michaell	The Good	The Duke	The Neptune	The Light
The Undertaker	The Faint hearted	The Moon	The Moderate	The Rainbow	Lotion
The Brave	The Pretious	The Trident	The Inconsiderate	The Indian	The Pretty
The Ambitious	The Aquillon	The Valiant	The Sea Horse	The Bizarre	The Palme
The Unparallell	The Fortune	The Bold	The Francois	The Solide	The Heady

Tenders and Fire Ships

Dutch

Red

28 Coronation Vice Admirall of the Blew Delavall S.	A Vtreght	Decker	I Mayd & Enhuyson Vander Poel	R Elswout	Nosthey
29 Katherine	Aulmer	B Mckenzen	Calf	K Noort Holland	Swaan	S Reygenberg	Van Zyl
30 Cambridge	Foulke	C Tholen	Calis	L Mayd & Dort	Pietersen	T Gewonden by Vice Adm.l Vander Putten
31 Berwick	Martin	D Westracer lane Vice Adm.l Calkenborgh	M Hollandia Lt. Adm.l Evertz en B C Toll
32 Swallow	Walters	E Princes	S B N Schey	N Veere	S B N	Brakell	W Veere	Meesdman
33 Defiance	Graydon	F Castruum	Cuyper	O Pro & Vovert	Convent	X Cortina	D Boon
34 Captaine	Jones	G Agatha	Vander saan	P D Maas	Snellen		
		H Senden lande	Taulman	Q Fria lant	Vander Gou		

of their probable behaviour, even in the unprecedently favourable situation in which they found themselves.

Although Torrington judged correctly, he had been ordered to fight. The impetuous spirit with which the Dutch in the van bore down was well expressed by one of their admirals, Schey. 'It was asked me', he wrote, 'if I saw it likely to beat so great a number with so few. I answered that this would not have been the first time we fought the French with half the number.' Schey thought little of the opposition, but the way in which the Dutch fought led them and the commander-in-chief into difficulties before a retreat was made good. If Tourville had pressed his advantage there could have been a disaster.

As it was, although the Dutch lost one ship taken in prize and others were so damaged that they had to be destroyed to save them

The British victory against the French off Barfleur, 19 May 1692.

from a similar fate, Torrington was able to preserve the rest to fight another day. He retreated in good order and Tourville did not harry him.

There was a major scandal when details became known in London and a court martial on Torrington was demanded. He escaped censure, as indeed he should have done, but he was not employed again at sea, for Orford supplanted him. The inquiry was one of a succession which did no good to the unity of the Navy, or to its public image. It was perhaps fortunate for Torrington that his encounter happened the day before the Battle of the Boyne, for the relief which was felt at the news from Ireland helped to blunt the severity with which the Admiral at one time seemed likely to be judged.

The following year was mostly taken up by the pacification of Ireland and when French and English met again at sea in strength, the conditions at Beachy Head were almost exactly reversed. This time, in May 1692 off Barfleur, it was Tourville who was heavily outnumbered. He had only forty-four ships to oppose the ninety-nine English and Dutch men-of-war which Orford had got together.

Tourville fought defensively with great distinction, but Orford did not allow his own advantage to be side-stepped and the French were scattered. During fighting which continued between 19 and 22 May, three ships were driven ashore on the rocky coast near Cherbourg, where they were set on fire by the English. They included Tourville's flagship, the *Soleil Royal*. Others, risking the dangerous navigation of the Alderney Race, reached Saint-Malo in safety, thanks to splendid pilotage by Hervé Riel. A third group reached the North Sea without serious misadventure, while a fourth, twelve in number, was overwhelmed and burnt by Sir George Rooke in the bay of La Hogue, on the eastern side of the Cherbourg Peninsula.

During the evening of 23 May, fire-ships and boats from Rooke's squadron swept in towards the shore. They made for six three-decked ships which were anchored under the protection of Fort Lisset. All were destroyed. On the opposite side of the bay the other vessels supposed themselves protected by the guns of Fort Saint-Vaast. They met their fate the next morning.

James II and his natural son the Duke of Berwick watched the scene from the shore. At one stage, when the second group of French ships were in danger, cavalrymen were ordered to the water's edge, to try to repel the seamen. They were dragged from their horses with boat-hooks. As a measure of finality, when the ships had been boarded and the crews driven away, the English sailors, before setting fire to their prizes, turned the guns against the fort, silencing it while last preparations went forward to ensure destruction. James is said to have remarked to Berwick: 'none but my brave English tars could have done so gallant a deed!' It was a matter on which he could speak with authority.

The destruction of the French flagship, the *Soleil Royal*, at La Hogue, 23 May 1692.

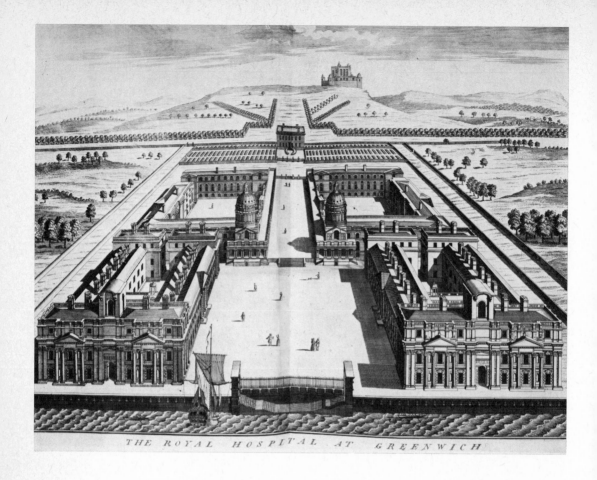

THE ROYAL HOSPITAL AT GREENWICH

Royal Hospital, Greenwich, in 1720.

A long succession of wars and successes have overlaid its impact, but Barfleur was considered by most contemporaries to have been the most impressive victory since the Armada, though the King complained that not enough had been done. Several HMS *Barfleur*s have adorned the Navy List and it was partly as a thank-offering, partly as a parallel gesture to the building of Wren's military hospital at Chelsea, that Queen Mary ordained that a hospital for seamen should be founded at Greenwich. There the Queen's House, the creation of Inigo Jones, already stood, together with a rambling palace. In 1694, shortly before Queen Mary's death, she and the King dedicated the place to the new purpose, a stipulation being made that a vista 115 feet wide should be preserved from the Inigo Jones building to the river. Wren was appointed architect and one of the grandest schemes of its kind in Europe began to take shape.

Samuel Johnson, who as a young man once lodged at Greenwich and who revered the place because of its associations, walked there in the park with his biographer in 1763, when pensioners had enjoyed their privileges for over half a century.

I was much pleased [Boswell related] to find myself with Johnson at Greenwich, which he celebrates in his *London*, as a favourite scene. I had the poem in my pocket, and read the lines aloud with enthusiasm.

> *On Thames's banks in silent thought we stood,*
> *Where Greenwich smiles upon the silver flood:*
> *Pleas'd with the seat which gave Eliza birth,*
> *We kneel, and kiss the consecrated earth.*

He remarked that the structure of Greenwich Hospital was too magnificent for a place of charity, and that its parts were too much detached to make one great whole.

Not all visitors to Greenwich have echoed Johnson, who sometimes talked for effect, though even he was impressed by the buildings which stand as a memorial to William and Mary. Although they are no longer a haven for the war-worn seamen, they continue to serve the purposes of the fleet. Since 1873 and thus, now, for a full century, the noble cluster has been used as the university of the Navy, a place for the higher education of its serving officers.

It so happened that the wish to prevent James from returning reinforced an important principle of English foreign policy: resistance against any ruler who aimed at complete supremacy on the Continent. This has long been familiar as the doctrine of the Balance of Power. While Louis XIV lived, he provided a ceaseless threat; and a characteristic of the eighteenth century as a whole is that for considerable stretches Britain was at war with France, or with Spain acting in French interests, or with the two countries together.

First rate ship in section, *c.* 1700. These large ships of the line were fitted as flagships, lesser rated ships forming the bulk of the fleet.

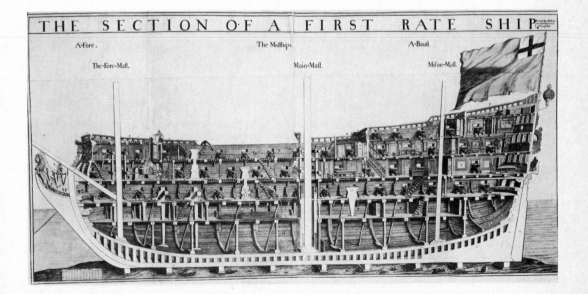

THE SECTION OF A FIRST RATE SHIP

A-Fore.   The Midships.   A-Baust.

The-Fore-Mast.   Main-Mast.   Mison-Mast.

In each succeeding war the Navy played a leading part and early in the century there were two considerable successes, in both of which Rooke commanded. The first was at Vigo in October 1702 when an Anglo-Dutch force, having failed in an attempt to take Cadiz, learnt that a Spanish treasure fleet had arrived from the West Indies, escorted by a French squadron.

Châteaurenault, the French Admiral, had thrown a boom across the inner harbour. This was covered by his own guns and those of the local forts. Sir Thomas Hopsonn destroyed the boom and troops assaulted the forts. The combined effort resulted in the loss of every ship not burnt by the French themselves. Rooke returned home with booty which included eleven million *pesos* or 'pieces of eight'. There still exist in collectors' cabinets many coins bearing the head of Anne, the new Queen of England, and the word 'Vigo'. Handsome compensation had been acquired for failure in the chief objective.

The second success was of more lasting importance. It was the capture of Gibraltar in 1704, a feat which was achieved a little short of a century after an event much celebrated in Holland, when Heemskirk destroyed ten Spanish galleons lying off the Rock. The Anglo-Dutch alliance, by then part of a greater combination, might, it seemed, emulate the achievements of an earlier epoch. At Gibraltar, victory was once again fortuitous, for Rooke's primary task had been an attack on Toulon. During the course of his eventful cruise he fought an action with the French off Malaga. Indecisive in itself, this saved Toulon, but it did not lead to the recapture of Gibraltar.

These moves were part of the War of the Spanish Succession, during the course of which Marlborough, by a series of victories, proved himself to be the greatest soldier living. The conflict itself had arisen from the fact that the King of Spain had died childless in 1700,

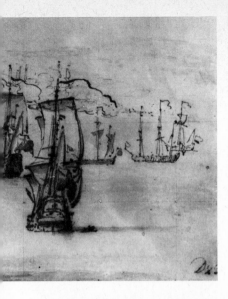

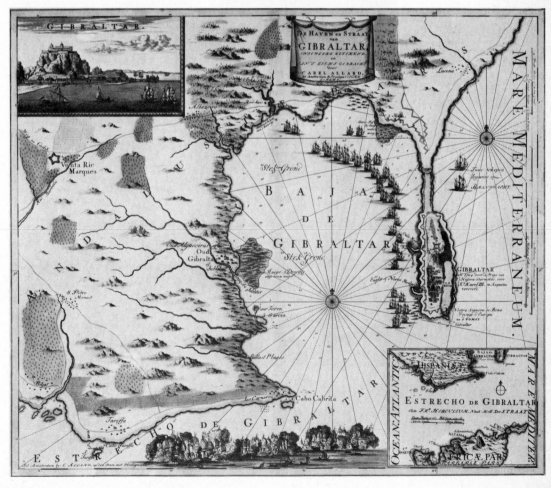

Admiral Sir John Leake:
painting by Sir Godfrey
Kneller.

bequeathing his dominions to Louis's grandson, Philip of Anjou.
The prospect of a Franco-Spanish hegemony appalled other European
princes and when, on the death of James II, the King of France
acknowledged the Pretender, William III joined with other sovereigns
in a decision to back a Habsburg candidate for the throne of Spain. A
Grand Alliance was formed, which included Austria, Prussia, the
Palatinate, Portugal and Savoy.

After William's death in 1702 his aims were pursued by Marlborough in the name of Queen Anne. Marlborough's strategy
concentrated on the use of land forces, but he recognized the value
of the Navy in a supporting role. One of his projects was to attack
the French in the Mediterranean, where they were vulnerable to the
pressure of sea power. What was needed was a base where a British
fleet could refit, without the need to return home each autumn. This
was not acquired until Sir John Leake and General Stanhope took
Minorca in 1708 and thereby had the use of the splendid harbour at
Port Mahon.

Leake, the son of a Master Gunner of England, has had less than
justice done him by posterity. He twice saved Gibraltar – once when
he relieved the garrison, which was under the command of the Prince
of Hesse, who had been left to defend it with a force of Marines;
and again in an action off Marbella in 1705. It is, incidentally, noteworthy that the Royal Marines, whose establishment on a permanent
basis dates from a later time, have 'Gibraltar' on their Colour in token
of prowess shown in every part of the world. The globe, encircled
with laurel, is itself their emblem.

The capture of Minorca: plan of Port Mahon, 1708.

By the Treaty of Utrecht, the provisions of which were formulated in 1713, Britain attained some of the objects for which she had fought. Louis, now in the last years of his life, acknowledged the Protestant succession, though he continued to sustain the exiled Stuarts, who made serious efforts to regain the throne of Britain, notably in 1715 and 1745. Louis's grandson Philip was confirmed in possession of the Spanish Empire, but a union of the French and Spanish crowns was prohibited. Gibraltar and Minorca were ceded to Britain by Spain, Minorca being relinquished later in the century. It was in the field of commercial and colonial interests that the treaty did least to ensure a permanent settlement, as subsequent wars indicated.

The country most discontented with the treaty was Spain. In 1718, as the result of an alliance between Britain, France and Austria against her, war recommenced, briefly. The Spanish wished to recover Sicily, which had been ceded to Austria, and a fleet was sent to the Mediterranean to prevent a change of sovereignty. Sir George Byng, making use of the facilities of Minorca, engaged a Spanish squadron near Messina. The action developed into a chase, in the course of which the Spanish flagship surrendered to Byng, who had sailed in the first of the *Barfleur*s. Sixteen ships were taken and seven burnt. The Navy was beginning to assume that although, given approximate equality in numbers, it could master the French, it had the opportunity to do even better against the Spaniards.

This led to over-confidence and to the revival of the belief, which had its origins in the days of Drake and Hawkins, that Spanish possessions overseas were ripe for the plucking. Admiral Vernon was said to have boasted that he could take Porto Bello, on the Isthmus of Panama, with six ships. When he succeeded, in 1739, the news was received in England for the spectacular achievement it was. But this was the last success of the kind, for when, in 1741, an attack was mounted against Cartagena, now part of Columbia, the affair was mishandled. Troops and seamen succumbed to disease in hundreds, as they always did when campaigning in the Spanish Main. The attacks were made during the course of the War of the Austrian Succession; though this was another dynastic struggle of which Britain took advantage at sea, she was not well prepared and the Navy was beginning to suffer from rigidity of tactics imposed from home.

Vernon was a man full of ideas. These included the important tenet, shared by thoughtful contemporaries, that the safety of the country in war depended upon the maintenance of a strong 'Western Squadron' to guard the approaches to the Channel. He proved the matter by denying essential supplies to the forces engaged by France to support the attempt of Prince Charles Edward Stuart to advance on London from Scotland, where he had obtained a strong position. The romantic adventure withered and the Prince became a fugitive. Vernon, having done his duty, disappeared into retirement, though not before he had added a new word to the language.

The taking of Porto Bello, 21–22 November 1739. The fleet won ten thousand dollars in Spanish treasure.

Admiral Edward Vernon.

Vernon's nickname among the seamen was 'old Grog', from his custom of wearing a grogram boat-cloak. In August 1740, at the height of his popularity, he was at Port Royal, Jamaica, with his flag in the *Burford*. It was from there that he wrote to the Admiralty to report numerous desertions, due to men 'stupefying themselves with spiritous Liquors'.

After consultation with captains and surgeons in the fleet, Vernon reported that he had 'ventured to attack that formidable Dagon,★ Drunkenness' by giving orders that the daily allowance of half a pint of rum per man be mixed with a quart of water, 'in one Scuttled Butt kept for that purpose, and to be done upon Deck and in the presence of the Lieutenant of the Watch', who would see to it that the men were not docked of their proper allowance. The Admiral added

★ Dagon, half man, half fish, was the god of the Philistines.

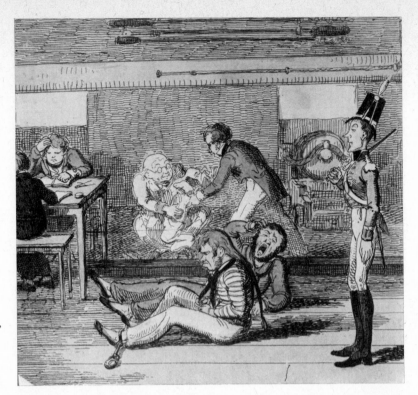

'In Irons for getting drunk.'
Lieutenant Sheringham
recorded a familiar scene in
this etching published by
Cruikshank.

that men 'that are good husbands may from the Savings of their Salt Provisions and Bread purchase Sugar and Limes to make the water more palatable to them'. A ceremony, similar to that devised in the West Indies so long ago, continued in the Navy until very recently. Many sailors, during the war then in progress and during others in the future, must have blessed Admiral Vernon, often without having the least idea who or what he was. Grog had indeed arrived, but, human nature being what it is, so had the state of being groggy.

Vernon was at one time acclaimed; but his influence never approached that of his contemporary, George Anson. Vernon had operated in the Caribbean; Anson emulated Drake in a circumnavigation, achieved between September 1740 and June 1744, which brought him wealth, celebrity and power. His original orders were to harry Spanish possessions in the Pacific. He flew a commodore's pendant in command of six ships of war and two victuallers. Only one, the sixty-gun flagship *Centurion*, was able to complete the voyage. The reason was partly weather, but above all the dreadful way in which the squadron had been manned. Anson was sent five hundred invalids to make up his numbers and two hundred raw Marines who had seen no service. Many of them succumbed before the mission was half over, all from sickness. In fact, during a voyage lasting nearly four years, four men were killed in action; over thirteen hundred died of scurvy.

Opposite: Admiral Lord
Anson, an engraving after
Sir Joshua Reynolds.

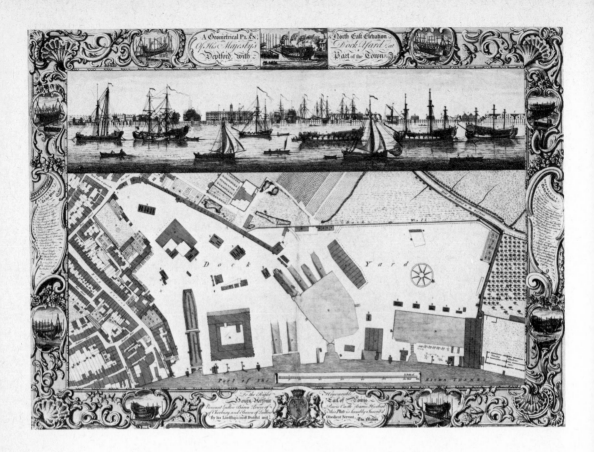

A Geometrical Plan of His Majesty's Deptford, with North East Elevation of the Dock Yard at Part of the Town

'His Majesty's Dockyard at Deptford', 1753.

The figures were not grossly out of scale with the usual mortality rate, during wartime, when scurvy and fever could ravage a fleet or an army. The reason was that the cause of scurvy, a deficiency in Vitamin C, was unknown. A few enlightened men had long discovered that the best anti-scorbutics included oranges and lemons (only one sort of lime was any use, and even that was not high on the list of remedials), but their example was overlooked or forgotten. Although a naval surgeon, James Lind, had by 1757 proved the matter beyond doubt in a series of dietetic experiments, it was not until 1795 that an official issue of lemon-juice was made to the fleet. Sad to say, in the middle of the nineteenth century the Admiralty substituted lime-juice because it was cheaper. There is, therefore, perhaps some justification for the scornful word 'limey' as applied to Englishmen.

Anson's trials abroad would have defeated most men, but he surmounted them all in a spirit of rational calm. His sailors won admiration from the Chinese for their courage in fire-fighting ashore at Canton. By then their spirits were high: on 20 June 1743, after a patient wait, they had intercepted, fought and captured the *Nuestra Señora de Covadonga*, a galleon laden with silver consigned from Acapulco to Manila. The treasure was transferred without loss and Anson, like Rooke before him, returned home rich for life. There was, however, a difference. Rooke, a Tory, had at the time the wrong political connections and in his last years suffered eclipse. Anson had the right ones, proving once again that political influence was a powerful aid to military success.

He was to become the son-in-law of Hardwicke, a Lord Chancellor, and from 1744 onwards he was at the centre of affairs. He became First Lord of the Admiralty; reorganized the Navy; encouraged George II to approve a uniform for officers; modernized the dock-yards; established the Marines on a permanent basis and rated the fighting ships in a more scientific scheme than before. At sea, he crowned his career by a victory over the French at a battle begun off Cape Finisterre in May 1747. The enemy was chased and during their retreat they lost four ships of the line, two frigates and seven merchant-men. Anson added to his wealth by substantial prize-money.

His best pupils were destined for high rank. It was said of Anson that 'he would go to any length to serve his friends, but was the reverse to those he had a dislike to.' The observation was true, but favoured officers, such as Saunders, Keppel, Philip Saumarez, Piercy Brett and Howe, who all made reputations either during the circum-navigation or later, were of uncommon ability. They had been chosen for their promise and they fulfilled it.

Not all of Anson's contemporaries were equally successful. Thomas Mathews was commander-in-chief of a fleet which was engaged with the French off Toulon in 1744. The result was indecisive in itself and led to serious consequences ashore in the land campaigns,

Toulon: 11 February 1744.

though Edward Hawke made his name on the occasion as a fighting man. Later, as a junior Rear-Admiral, Hawke repeated Anson's success in another 'chase' action off Ushant, only six months after the earlier victory. The French Admiral, L'Etenduére, lost nine ships of war and Hawke was given a knighthood.

The affair off Toulon produced a series of courts martial, including one on Mathews and another on Lestock, his second-in-command, who, so it was alleged, had not properly supported his chief. The two were on the worst of terms and both had explosive tempers, Mathews being known as 'Il Furibondo'. Politics influenced the proceedings: Lestock was acquitted while Mathews was dismissed the service. Lestock was a Whig and to the end of his life Mathews, who was of a different persuasion, regarded the outcome as outrageous. What was beyond a shade of doubt was that the recriminations which followed the action did no good to the Navy.

This was all the sadder since, mainly by the vision, dedication and reforms of two men, Pepys and Anson, in successive generations, the Navy had by now not only become fully integrated, as well as reasonably well equipped by the standards of the time, but was also seen by those in power as the principal *permanent* instrument whereby the country's foreign policy could be effected or supported. The national prejudice against standing armies was far too strong ever to be eradicated; similarly, although both William III and Anne maintained large military forces to sustain what was to become a protracted struggle against France, without being able to rely upon the services of a strong navy, they could not have hoped to employ any scheme of grand strategy with a chance of success.

It is true that, after the exodus of James II, the supervision of the fleet was never again so closely a personal concern of the sovereign and that the office of Lord High Admiral was for the most part in commission, that is to say, its powers were exercised by a Board of Admiralty. Yet while the sovereign's influence continued to be a major factor in foreign policy, the state of the fleet continued to be of direct concern to those who occupied the throne.

Chapter Four

THE SEVEN YEARS WAR

The War of the Austrian Succession had one important result for the Navy: it halted the process of decline which had set in after Utrecht – the seemingly inevitable accompaniment to a period of relative peace. Yet in a military and political sense, the war, which ended in 1748 at the Treaty of Aix-la-Chapelle, settled even less than usual. This was particularly true across the Atlantic, where the rivalry of French and British was as acute as it was in India.

Britain made a serious error, so far as her North American interests were concerned, by restoring the naval base at Louisbourg, on Cape Breton Island, to France. The fortress had been captured mainly by the efforts of the colonists, who were not consulted as to the terms of the Peace. Louisbourg, situated near the entrance to the St Lawrence, guarded the sea route to the interior of Canada. It could also be used by forces engaged in attacking the huge volume of shipping plying between Britain and the ports of the eastern coast of America.

Hostilities developed between British and French long before a state of war was formally declared, for the frontier was in a state of perpetual flux. By their design of building a chain of forts between Louisiana and the Great Lakes, along the line of the Ohio, the French, so it was perceived, intended to confine the British colonists to the area east of the Allegheny Mountains. The expansionist pressures of more than a million British colonists thus seemed threatened.

During the course of what became known as the Seven Years War (1756–63), the Navy attained a new peak of renown, revealing as never before the value of a maritime strategy in the struggle for empire. When the conflict opened, Anson, who had been born in the seventeenth century, still presided over the Admiralty. Before it ended, Nelson had joined a lively brood of children in the nursery of a Norfolk parsonage.

At the outset of war, Minorca came under siege. Admiral Byng, a son of the victor of Passaro, was sent to relieve it. He failed and the island surrendered. There was such an outcry that on his return Byng was arrested, confined and tried, as if he had been a conspirator rather than a commander who had not been well supported at home, the best ships having been allotted to the Channel.

What had happened was that there had come a moment in a confused action with a French fleet when Byng, if he had abandoned a rigid line formation at an early stage, as his flag-captain suggested, might have routed the enemy. Unhappily, Byng had sat on Mathews's court martial and dolefully replied: 'Remember the misfortunes of Mr Mathews.' Then events had moved fast and Byng actually did leave the line in a desperate effort to redeem the day. He was too late. Many of his ships were damaged in masts and spars, for the French, as usual, aimed high with this very purpose. They made good their retreat and Byng, after summoning a council of war, decided to return home, leaving Minorca to its fate. No ships had been lost on either side.

The inevitable court martial found Byng guilty, under the Articles of War by which the Navy was then regulated, of 'not doing his utmost to take or destroy the enemy's ships'. He was acquitted of cowardice or disaffection, but the Article in question carried the death penalty and the court had no choice but to pronounce it. Its verdict, signed and dated on board the *St George* in Portsmouth Harbour on 27 January 1757, included the following honourable sentences addressed to the Admiralty:

Right: Admiral John Byng,
1749.

Below: Louisbourg,
commanding the entrance
to the St Lawrence, 1731.

The execution of Admiral Byng, on board the *Monarque*, 1757: 'I heartily wish the shedding of my Blood may contribute to the Happiness and Service of my Country. . . .'

We cannot help laying the Distresses of our Minds before your Lordships, on this occasion, in finding ourselves under a Necessity of condemning a Man to Death, from the great Severity of the 12th Article of War, part of which he falls under; and which admits of no Mitigation, *even if the Crime should be committed by an Error in Judgment only*. And therefore, for our Consciences' sake, as well as in justice to the Prisoner, We pray Your Lordships in the most earnest manner, to recommend Him to His Majesty's Clemency.

George II, to his everlasting shame, refused the 'Clemency' asked, and Byng was shot. There had been no worse legalistic crime in the nation's annals. Voltaire's acid comment was justified. In England, so he wrote in *Candide*, it is thought well to kill an admiral from time to time – 'pour encourager les autres'.

A war begun in such a way did not, so it might have seemed, deserve to prosper: but in the same year William Pitt, who had pleaded for Byng, took office as Secretary of State. He proved to be the greatest war minister Britain had yet found.

The country had an ally in Prussia, the ruler of which was Frederick the Great. Because he was Elector of Hanover, if for no other reason, George II favoured a continental policy. An army was maintained to aid Frederick, who was also subsidized with cash. The soldiers did not add much to their laurels and even Frederick, military genius that he was, became at times hard pressed, faced with Austria as well as France for his enemy.

It was partly to divert forces which might otherwise be used against Prussia, but still more because he believed in it for itself, that Pitt favoured a maritime strategy. This would make use of Britain's naval strength, and so would reflect Francis Bacon's observation, made as early as the era of Elizabeth: 'this much is certain: that he who commands the sea is at great liberty, and may take as much and as little of the war as he will'. Pitt would make use of surprise; and so far as the draining of French resources was concerned, he would win the war in America.

There were setbacks before the difficult science of Combined Operations was mastered, but in the end British dominance in this sphere came to be accepted. The successive stages through which satisfactory co-operation between Navy and Army was achieved may be illustrated by operations which were mounted in 1757 against Rochefort, in the following year against Louisbourg and in 1759 against Quebec, in each of which James Wolfe took part. The first expedition, in which the admiral was Hawke, was a total failure, the only officer to gain credit being Howe, who set a fine example in the *Magnanime* by silencing French forts. Wolfe remarked that:

> Experience shows me that, in an affair depending upon vigour and despatch, the generals should settle their plan of operations, so that no time may be lost in idle debate and consultations when the sword should be drawn; that pushing on smartly is the road to success, and more particularly so in an affair of this nature; that nothing is to be reckoned an obstacle to your undertaking which is not found really so upon *tryal*; that in war something must be allowed to chance and fortune, seeing it is in its nature hazardous, and an option of difficulties; that the greatness of an object should come under consideration, opposed to the impediments that lie in the way.

The taking of Louisbourg on Cape Breton Island, 1758: part of Pitt's great plan to win Canada from the French.

Against Louisbourg, the admiral was Edward Boscawen, the general being Amherst, with Wolfe as his second. The great fortified base on Cape Breton Island fell once more to British forces, this time mainly from home. It was retained at the peace though its bastions were slighted, for its threat diminished after the establishment of a rival base at Halifax, Nova Scotia.

Quebec fell to Wolfe in September of what became known as the 'Year of Victories', 1759, when Garrick sang 'Heart of Oak' to enraptured audiences, Boscawen won a sea victory off Lagos and Hawke a still more resounding one in Quiberon Bay, while British infantry under Ferdinand of Brunswick gained lasting renown at Minden.

The operations which cost Wolfe his life in the moment of victory on the Heights of Abraham were in many ways extraordinary. Success could not have been achieved without the tireless services of Sir Charles Saunders, one of Anson's ablest admirals. He took his ships up the St Lawrence in face of navigational difficulties which had been thought insurmountable. He sent Marines ashore to fight with the Army. He backed Wolfe's brigadiers in their opinion that an assault should be made from above rather than from below the city; and he found a junior officer, James Chads, who fulfilled the near-miraculous task of leading a boat convoy thirteen miles down a fast-flowing tidal river in darkness, and setting the troops ashore in the right place.

Among the naval contingent was James Cook, the future hydrographer-explorer, who was then sailing-master in the *Pembroke*; also John Jervis, at that time a commander, but one day to become

The landing, the ascent of the cliffs and the battle on the Heights of Abraham shown as one action: the capture of Quebec in 1759 was a brilliant advertisement for the value of combined operations.

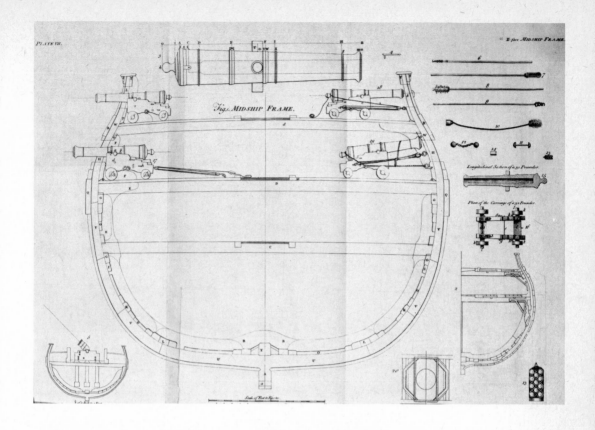

Midship section of a man-of-war, 1769, showing guns in board (*right*) and run out for firing (*left*).

Admiral the Earl of St Vincent. Montcalm had among his French officers the Comte de Bougainville, who in later years was to win celebrity as a circumnavigator. Wolfe and Saunders seized what Wolfe called 'the lucky moment in war' and although Quebec was in some danger the following winter, the return of the Navy, once the St Lawrence was ice-free, ensured relief and, in due course, the conquest of all Canada.

Combined operations had necessitated special craft for landings. There had been no startling progress in general ship design since the heyday of the Pett family, but the development of flat-bottomed boats for amphibious warfare, employed with much effect at Quebec and elsewhere, was of importance in showing how war may quicken invention.

The method of use of these new craft was described by a German visitor, Frederick Kielmansegge, when further expeditions were preparing:

Since the beginning of this war the English have very much accelerated the embarkation and disembarkation of troops by inventing for the purpose a kind of flat boat, in which my Lord Howe has taken a considerable part. These boats are arranged for fifty or sixty men; their shape is somewhat similar to that of the long boats which men-of-war generally carry, but they are much larger and have flat bottoms for the purpose of getting closer into shore.

All of these flat boats, each of which has twenty to twenty-one oars, were lying in one row along the shore, and as soon as the regiment had marched past it formed up again close to the shore, and awaited the signal for entering the boats. Immediately on this being given, each officer marched with his men to the boat, of which he had previously received the number; then he and his drummer entered first and passed right through from the bows onshore to the stern, the whole division following him without breaking their ranks; so that in two minutes everybody was in the boats.

The officers and drummers, with their corporals, sit aft near the rudder, the privates in two or three rows behind one another on the thwarts, holding their muskets before them, and two petty officers sit in the bows, so as not to be hampered in the use of their oars. As soon as everything has been arranged in this way, the naval officer commanding the embarkation gives a signal, when all the boats start off at the same time and row to their respective vessels.

Such methods were employed in the West Indies, both before and after Spain had joined in the war at the side of France. In 1762 the Spanish lost Havana, where enormous prize-money was collected by Sir George Pocock, the Admiral concerned, by Keppel, his second, and by the General, Lord Albemarle, who happened to be head of the Keppel family. Even in the preliminary distribution the commanders-in-chief received £70,000 apiece, as against £4 1s 8½d for a private soldier and £3 14s 9¾d for a blue-jacket, and much more followed. Manila also fell to an amphibious force organized from India, although the Philippines have been so long associated with the United States that this is often forgotten. Pocock had earlier fought three severe actions in Indian waters, by which he obtained strategic control in the Far East.

As for the more straightforward maritime encounters of the war, during August 1759 Boscawen chased de la Clue, whose fleet was based on Toulon, but who was in the process of transferring his force westward as part of an ambitious concentration aimed at the invasion of Britain. Boscawen drove five ships to take refuge in the bay of Lagos, where two were wrecked and three were captured.

Hawke's victory, the last of the year, took place in November, in an autumn of storms. It was of Handelian grandeur and in sheer excitement has possibly never been matched. His opponent was Conflans, who was to have had charge of the main fleet covering an invading army. He had no chance while the British fleet remained in being. At Quiberon, Hawke – who had taken 'Strike' for his motto – made his close blockade of the western ports of France serve as the prelude to an annihilation of a kind that was later so well understood by Nelson.

Stress of weather had at one time forced the commander-in-chief to take the big ships back to Torbay. The wind being right for him, Conflans then seized the moment to put to sea. He was shadowed by

Captain Robert Duff, whom Hawke had left in charge of a detachment for that purpose. Conflans gave chase, but before long he was warned by his look-outs that Hawke had returned. Conflans recalled his ships, intending to take them back to their anchorage in an orderly way. Hawke had other ideas.

To the amazement of the French, who knew that he had no local pilots, Hawke signalled to his captains to follow the enemy in among the rocks and shoals of an iron coast. When the master of the *Royal George*, the fleet flagship, ventured to question such temerity, Hawke remarked: 'You have done your duty in pointing out the danger.' He added that where the French could go, he could follow, and that he intended to get alongside the *Soleil Royal*, which wore Conflan's flag. Conflans himself, in the despatch which he wrote after the battle, said: 'I had no reason to believe that if I went in first with my ships, the enemy would dare to follow, in spite of his superiority, which would in any case confine his movements in such a limited area.'

Howe in the *Magnanime*, as ever to the fore, led the ships of the line, though in crowding on sail, his main topgallant-yard was carried away. While parties went aloft, to make good the damage, Howe told the rest to attend closely to orders and to 'keep back their fire till they could put their hands to the muzzles of the enemy's guns'. This was an uncharacteristic piece of exaggeration, but the men knew perfectly well what Howe meant.

The signal for close action was seen flying from the *Royal George* at about half past two on a gloomy afternoon, in a high sea, with not many hours of daylight left. By four o'clock, the *Formidable* had struck her colours. Shortly afterwards the *Superbe* foundered. Next to suffer was the *Thésée*. Opening her lower gun-ports in the heavy weather, she allowed water to rush in; the ship then filled, capsized and sank.

'Night was now come', wrote Hawke in his despatch, 'and being on a part of the coast, among islands and shoals, of which we were totally ignorant . . . and blowing hard on a lee shore, I made the signal to anchor.' All through the night that followed, signals of distress lit the darkness, and so did flames from burning vessels. The *Heros* and the *Soleil Royal* had taken the ground, as had the *Juste*. The first two were destroyed; the *Juste* broke up; but the victors also suffered. The *Resolution* lay dismasted on Four Bank and the *Essex* was lost in going to her help.

The main body of the French crept into the mouth of the Vilaine, except for five under the Chevalier de Beauffremont-Listenois, who managed to escape to Rochefort. The French fleet was eliminated as a coherent force, and the final words on his magnificent feat should be given to Hawke himself.

> When I consider the season of the year, the hard gales on the day of action, a flying enemy, the shortness of the day, and the coast they were on, I can boldly affirm that all that could possibly be done has been done.

As for the loss we have sustained, let it be placed to the account of the necessity I was under of running all risks to break this strong force of the enemy.

George II died in 1760 and after his grandson had succeeded to the throne as George III, Pitt did not long survive as the architect of victory. This mattered less than it would have done a few years earlier, for Britain's position was such that she could negotiate from strength. She did so at the Peace of Paris, which confirmed her in the possession of those territories overseas which she deemed most useful to her – Canada, certain West Indian islands, Senegal; and Minorca, the cause of the tragedy of Admiral Byng.

The young King, whose very long reign was to compass all the remaining feats achieved by the sailing navy, was the most cultivated of men. His enthusiasm for science and navigation led him to acquire a fine library on these and other subjects, and his encouragement of exploration, channelled through the Royal Society, led to an enormous advance in European knowledge of the Pacific. In this, the Navy played an essential part, and the unique qualities possessed by James Cook were given thorough scope.

Cook was a very rare instance of what merit could achieve in an age of privilege. The son of a farm labourer, this Yorkshireman served in colliers before volunteering for the Navy. His gifts were recognized and within a few years he became a warrant officer. After serving with the fleet at Quebec, he was engaged in a survey of the St Lawrence which won general admiration. His successive captains became his partisans and one of them, Palliser, had influence on the Board of Admiralty. In 1768 it was decided by the Royal Society to send an expedition to Tahiti, which had recently been discovered by Captain Samuel Wallis, to observe a transit of Venus across the sun. Cook was given a commission as lieutenant and put in command of the *Endeavour*, a ship built on the lines of the Whitby colliers he had known since childhood. With the *Endeavour* sailed Sir Joseph Banks, a rich amateur botanist to whom is owed not only a lively account of Cook's first circumnavigation, but an incidental picture of the man himself. During the voyage (1768–71) Cook charted the coasts of New Zealand, the east coast of Australia and part of New Guinea, though he did not find the hoped-for southern continent and the expedition was also somewhat disappointing in the sphere of astronomical observations.

Cook sailed again in 1772, this time in the *Resolution*, with another ship, the *Adventure*, in company. He skirted Antarctica, pushing further south than any earlier explorer, and confirmed that the elusive continent did not exist. His record of health was remarkable but he did not, as some have claimed, 'conquer scurvy'. He was not in much danger from it, for his ships were exceptionally well provisioned, and Cook took every chance to replenish with fresh food.

On his third and last voyage, begun in 1776 when he had reached the rank of post captain, Cook discovered what he named the

Captain James Cook; oil
painting by John Webber.

Sandwich Islands, in honour of the First Lord of the Admiralty. He
sailed as far north in the Pacific as possible before being stopped by
ice, and returning to the Sandwich Islands, now known as Hawaii,
he was killed in a fracas with the natives.

Cook's principal memorial is the map of the world's largest ocean;
and as Australia and New Zealand were populated later by people of
British stock, he extended the Empire far beyond the scope of any
single predecessor, although the fact was not apparent at the time.
His genius lay partly in his ceaseless curiosity. 'The world will hardly
admit an excuse for a man leaving a Coast unexplored he has once

Captain Cook lands in the New Hebrides on his second great voyage.

'A White Bear', illustration from *Voyage to the Pacific*, 1784.

discovered,' he wrote. He himself was impelled 'not only to go further than any one had done before, but as far as it was possible for a man to go'.

In a sense, his three voyages were the most remarkable feats achieved by one man in any navy at any time. In his personal career, he exemplified how far the British Navy had come since the time of the Tudors. It had shown challenge once again, and it had extended exploration.

Cook learnt his profession, like Drake before him, in trading-vessels. He enlisted in the Navy because, with remarkable acumen, he saw in it a path of advancement which no trader could offer. To the Navy, by means of a series of enlightened captains, belongs the credit of making the most of the man they had acquired. His advance was steady, and every step of it earned: able seaman; master's mate; master – that is, with the status of warrant officer – then commissioned rank, first as lieutenant and finally as post captain.

The hydrographer–explorer learnt surveying in Canada from military men, chiefly from Samuel Jan Holland and Joseph des Barres, who both served with him in the expedition to Quebec led by Saunders and Wolfe. After his second voyage, the Navy rewarded him with a captaincy of Greenwich Hospital. Cook was suitably gratified, but he had this to say about the appointment:

> A few months ago the whole Southern Hemisphere was hardly enough for me, and now I am going to be confined within the narrow limits of Greenwich Hospital, which are far too small for an active mind like mine. I must confess it is a fine retreat, and a pretty income, but whether I can bring myself to like ease and retirement time will show.

Time did show, for Cook was off on his final voyage soon after these words were written. Yet, had he never gone to sea again, he would already have done enough to be assured of fame and even perhaps of the statue which now stands in his commemoration near Admiralty Arch in the Mall. Although Cook did much, by his work and example, to show that the Navy could hold fine prospects for a man, humbly born, who had the necessary ability, the Navy, and indeed the sovereign himself, were not slow to recognize the outstanding qualities which Cook possessed.

Chapter Five

THE NAVY IN ADVERSITY

The high strain of the later phases of the Seven Years War was not sustained. By the time of Cook's death the Navy, like the nation, was deep in adversity. It was in process of losing the American colonies and was about to face France and Spain, both set upon revenging past humiliations.

It could not even be said that the service itself was united. 'An officer has nothing to do with political discussions or speculative opinions concerning government', said Sir John Lawson, an Admiral of the old Dutch wars who changed allegiance from Commonwealth to King. 'His first and only object ought to be to serve his country.' This was a counsel of perfection seldom realized between 1775 and 1783, the years of the conflict with America. The trouble arose not only from party divisions, which were as sharp as ever, but because there were deep differences of view as to how the Americans should be treated. Some were for conciliation and concession. Others, including those in power, insisted on coercion. The attempt at force failed; the colonists won their independence. In the long run the break was inevitable; for the Navy, however, it meant the loss of a valuable source of supplies at a time when corruption, conservatism and rigidity of tactics hampered its effectiveness.

At the outset, Lord Howe and his soldier brother Sir William Howe commanded the British forces. Lord Howe managed his fleet with exceptional skill and Sir William, who had been with Wolfe at Quebec, won a costly victory at Bunker Hill. But the Howes found they could not come to terms with the colonists and they became increasingly out of sympathy with the home government. In 1778 they handed over responsibility to others and it was four years before Lord Howe consented to serve again at sea.

The French came into the war in 1778 and the Spaniards followed a year later. At sea, there were four main areas of operations – the Channel and its approaches; the West Indies and east coast of North America; the Far East; and Gibraltar. As regards the main fleets, the

Lord Howe, wax relief by
John Flaxman.

war began with an inconclusive engagement, out in the Atlantic,
between Keppel and Orvilliers, a typical case where two large fleets
met, cannonaded and then went their several ways, with damage
on both sides but nothing decided. Keppel, so he thought, was ill
supported by Admiral Palliser, Cook's patron, and although he did
not at first express his dissatisfaction, he refused Palliser's request that
he should publicly vindicate his conduct. Courts martial followed.
They split the Navy, as all such inquiries were apt to do. Keppel was
acquitted, amid general rejoicing, for he was as popular as Vernon
had once been. In his turn, Palliser was exonerated, but the mob
broke his windows.

As neither Keppel nor Howe could or would serve, the Channel
fleet was given to a succession of ancient or undistinguished flag-
officers, Sir Francis Geary, Sir Charles Hardy and George Darby.
They were lucky in two respects, first because a preponderant
Franco-Spanish fleet made no use of a great opportunity, second

Rear-Admiral Richard
Kempenfelt; oil painting
by the American Ralph
Earl.

because they had Rear-Admiral Richard Kempenfelt as Captain of the
Fleet or Chief of Staff. Kempenfelt, and his friend Sir Charles Middleton, later Lord Barham, were among the most thoughtful officers of
their time. Kempenfelt helped to transform the signal system then
in use and when, for a brief period, he was given an independent
squadron, he captured a vital convoy under the very nose of the
escort, which consisted of the pick of the French navy. 'There is a
vulgar notion', he once wrote, 'that our seamen are braver than the
French. Ridiculous to suppose courage dependent upon climate. The
men who are best disciplined, of whatever nationality they are,
will always fight the best. . . . It is a maxim that experience has ever
confirmed, that discipline gives more force than numbers.'

Kempenfelt had served for some considerable time in the Far East
earlier in his life. It was there, during the War of American Independence, that the Royal Navy, represented by Sir Edward Hughes,
fought a series of fierce duels with the Bailli de Suffren, which

Romulus, a fifth rate taken by the French in Chesapeake Bay, February 1781, in an isolated action.

recalled the course of similar actions, tactically indecisive, between Admirals Pocock and d'Aché during the Seven Years War. Suffren was recognized on both sides as the best and boldest tactician that the French navy ever produced. Had he been properly supported by his captains he would never have allowed Hughes to repeat Pocock's feat of maintaining strategic control in Indian waters. Even so, Hughes had a hard struggle and the principal clashes did not occur until a later stage in the war.

It was on the far side of the Atlantic that the most significant naval movements took place, for not only was the conflict concerned with the future control of North America, but it would also affect that of the West Indies. The Caribbean islands, which had attracted settlers ever since Sir Thomas Warner claimed St Kitts in the reign of James I, had become of immense importance as a source of wealth to various nations, notably Spain, France and Britain, and to a much lesser degree, Holland and Denmark. In every war involving Britain, France and Spain it became an operational area.

The wind conditioned campaigning. The constant factor was the trade wind, which from November to April blew from a little to the north of east. From May until October it veered round almost to due east and in the later months of this period hurricanes could be expected. Large-scale operations were not then attempted; the fleets proceeded north or returned to Europe. It was in September 1781 that an action was fought which decided the future course of the war. As Washington himself admitted, it was a principal factor through which American independence was gained.

As so often, the battle itself was tactically indecisive. The British Admiral, Graves, came upon the French in Chesapeake Bay. He

decided to attack, but not in Hawke's fashion. He kept so rigidly to the formal rules that de Grasse, the French Admiral, was allowed to regain his anchorage without loss, after desultory manœuvring in the Atlantic which lasted some days. Graves had to withdraw to repair damage, which meant that General Cornwallis, whose army ashore was awaiting supplies and support from the fleet, was forced to surrender. Graves's second-in-command, Sir Samuel Hood, was loud in his criticism of how the engagement had been conducted: but he himself had shown no initiative whatever during the critical stages. It was perhaps fortunate that this time there were no courts martial, despite the gravity of the general situation.

The relief of Gibraltar, 1781; painting by Dominic Serres.

Redeeming episodes in an otherwise disappointing war concerned Gibraltar and the West Indies. The Admiralty, hard pressed to find capable admirals willing to serve an unpopular ministry, offered the West Indian command to the veteran Rodney. He was embarrassed by debt, in poor health and, at that time, abroad: but a French friend, Marshal Biron, lent Rodney the money necessary for him to return to England, after consulting the Minister of Marine. This dignitary agreed to the transaction, adding that in his opinion naval actions were of no consequence. 'It is piff-poff on one side and the other,' he remarked, 'and afterwards the sea is just as salt!' This was an astounding observation from one who had supervision over the second navy in Europe, but not untypical of a country which always placed its sea service second to its land forces.

Rodney's first assignment was to relieve Gibraltar, which between 1779 and 1783 underwent its sternest siege. The defence was conducted in a masterly way by General Eliott, later Lord Heathfield. The Spaniards regarded it as a matter of honour to recapture the

The sinking of the *Royal George* at Spithead, 29 August 1782.

Rock and the French gave them every support. The fortress was thrice supplied and reinforced from the sea, an undertaking requiring a powerful fleet to cover the merchantmen.

In 1780 Rodney was the Admiral concerned. In the following year it was Darby, and in 1782, Howe, back at last among his sailors. The second and third sorties resulted in no serious general engagement, although Howe considered the feat to be the most difficult of his life. He had a sad start, for when his ships were assembling at Spithead, the *Royal George*, which had been Hawke's flagship at Quiberon and was flying the blue flag of Richard Kempenfelt, filled and sank when undergoing a small repair, drowning the Admiral and hundreds of those on board, including civilians. The Court of Inquiry decided that the ship's timbers were rotten and it is possible that, had she sailed, she might have foundered at sea, with still greater loss of life. At the time, there was a timber famine in the dockyards, and repairs were scamped.

Rodney's experience as he made his way to Gibraltar provided heartening proof that his capacity was as considerable as ever and it cheered the nation in a period of justified gloom. Off Finisterre he snapped up a valuable Spanish convoy, sixteen merchantmen all told, and he also captured the escorting men-of-war, six in number. Then, in a night action during a January gale off Cape St Vincent, he took further men-of-war including the flagship of Admiral de Langara. Rodney had one of the royal princes in his fleet, William

Henry. Half a century later he came to the throne as William IV, and he was always to remember with pride his initiation into naval warfare.

Rodney belonged to the generation which had learnt from Anson and Hawke. Although confined by illness to his cot, it was not surprising that during what became known as the 'Moonlight Battle' he ordered a general chase, and hoisted the signal for engaging to leeward so as to prevent the enemy from running into Cadiz. In addition to five prizes, the *Santo Domingo* caught fire and blew up, and other Spanish ships were wrecked. The British greatly benefited from having their ships' bottoms lined with copper, a practice which had been begun experimentally in 1761. 'Without them', wrote Rodney, 'we should not have taken one Spanish ship.' 'Coppering' was in fact one of the major technical improvements to the Navy of the era.

When Rodney reached the Caribbean after his exploits in the Atlantic, he was faced by de Guichen, who had a large force at his disposal and who intended to keep it intact. He succeeded, although

Prince William Henry, later William IV, on board the *Royal George*, under instruction by Admiral Digby.

Admiral Lord Rodney by
Sir Joshua Reynolds.

Rodney might have inflicted a defeat on him in April 1780 off
Martinique had he been supported more intelligently, or had his
subordinates understood his intentions more clearly. These were to
bring a preponderant strength to bear against a portion only of the
enemy line and thus ensure at the very least a limited victory.

'The painful task of thinking belongs to me', he wrote afterwards
to Rear-Admiral Rowley, who in Rodney's view had played a less
than satisfactory part in the encounter. It is perhaps a fair criticism of
the commander-in-chief that he did not always make his thoughts
plain enough to those who were expected to carry them out.

War was declared on Holland in December 1780, the reason being
the help given by Dutch traders to the Americans, for which purpose their island possession of St Eustacius, situated to the north-
west of St Kitts, was invaluable. Rodney was able to capture this
entrepôt together with an immense haul of goods, but the affair
led to trouble of every kind from the merchants who suffered –
traitorous British ones included. Sir Samuel Hood, who had become
Rodney's second-in-command, considered, with some reason, that
the glittering prospect of prize-money adversely affected Rodney's
strategic judgment.

Opposite above: the
surrender of St Eustacius to
Rodney, 3 April 1781.

Opposite below: plan of the
Dogger Bank action,
5 August 1781, by an
officer on the spot. 'Blast
my Eyes Get Back in the
Texel', the English sailor
tells his Dutch counterpart.

The break with Holland also led to the first of the only two set-
piece battles between old rivals at sea which occurred in the eighteenth
century. It was fought in August 1781 near the Dogger Bank. The
British commander was Sir Hyde Parker the elder, a crusted character
noted rather for ill temper than for tactical skill, and an officer for
whom no words from Rodney, under whom he had served, were too
harsh. The result was a typical slogging match, with no finesse on
either side – just what Rodney would have expected from Parker.

Rodney himself ended a very long career in a blaze of glory, not
in the slightest dimmed when he learnt that the government, just

A SCETCH of the ENGAGEMENT under the COMMAND of VICE ADMIRAL PARKER on the DOGGER BANK with the DUTCH SQUADREN of much Superior force Aug.st 5 1781.

Drawn by an Officer on the Spot.

A. the Fortitude.
B. the Princess Amelia.
C. the Berwick.
D. the Bienfaisant.
E. the Buffalo.
F. the Preston.
G. the Dolphin.

X. the Dutch Adm.l.
I. the Fleet of Dutch.
O. the Dutch Convoy.
Q. 1 74 Dutch Ship sunk in 22 fathom Water.

Blast my Eyes Get Back in the Texel.

I'm sinking.

before they had news of his triumph, had dispatched a most undistinguished man to take over his command. In the spring of 1782 he
faced de Grasse, who maintained de Guichen's principle of avoiding
close action whenever an object could be attained without it. The
Frenchman hoped to be the means of a successful invasion of Jamaica,
which since Cromwell's time had been firmly in British possession.
His plan was to join up with the Spanish forces in Haiti and then to
complete the business.

Rodney and Hood were far too alert, experienced and skilful to
allow any such possibility to be realized. When one of de Grasse's
ships, the *Zélée*, had the misfortune to suffer two separate collisions,
requiring fleet support to save her from capture, de Grasse accepted
the risk of the mêlée he had long striven to avoid. The result was an
action of precisely the kind for which Rodney had hoped ever since
the disappointing encounter of April 1780. It became known to
history as the Battle of 'the Saints', after the island passage where
most of the fighting took place.

The two fleets were already in close action when a shift of wind
enabled some of Rodney's captains to break through the enemy line,
thus isolating individual ships and preventing their escape. By sunset
on 12 April 1782 a victory was crowned by the surrender of de Grasse
in his splendid flagship the *Ville de Paris*. The French commander-
in-chief lowered his colours to Hood in the *Barfleur*, a successor to
the ship which had carried Byng's flag at Cape Passaro. James
Saumarez, who commanded the *Russell* and had only joined Rodney's

Rodney breaking the line
at the Battle of 'the Saints',
1782.

line at the last moment, had a hand in this most important capture.

Hood was for pressing on against a scattered and disheartened foe, but Rodney said to him next day: 'Come, we have done very handsomely as it is' – a remark which would never have satisfied Hawke, or Nelson, or even Rodney himself when younger. It was excusable in a tired but elated man.

Rodney's Captain of the Fleet, Sir Charles Douglas, by improving the traverse of the guns and by his attention to the speed of firing, played a great part in the day. In writing to his friend Sir Robert Keith, the British Ambassador at Vienna, he used the word 'incision' to describe how the French line had been confused and routed.

Also on board Rodney's flagship, the *Formidable*, was his physician, Sir Gilbert Blane, who had been a disciple of James Lind. It was almost entirely due to Blane that the health of the fleet on a station notorious for sickness was markedly better than usual. The seamen were given the benefit of spruce beer, which Saunders and Wolfe had found to be efficacious in Canada years before; and it is significant that Rodney himself had a lemon constantly in his hand and often at his lips. A martyr to gout, at least he would never succumb to scurvy. Blane, to whom much medical reform was due, both then and later, was also noted for his attention to the better ventilation of ships, a crucial matter on tropical stations.

One other member of the Admiral's entourage deserves remark, James Sidney Yorke, a midshipman aged fourteen. The day after the battle he wrote to his uncle, the second Lord Hardwicke, telling him:

I sit down with the greatest Pleasure imaginable to tell you the joyful News which I am sure must give an Englishman pleasure to hear, a Victory over the French which is Equal to that of La Hogue. We have stopped all the Proceedings of the French against Jamaica. We have taken burnt and sunk 6 Sail of the Line. The *Ville de Paris* of 110 guns struck to us, and Sir Charles Douglas went on board of her and said that the *Formidable* was a Bomb Boat to her. De Grasse is a prisoner on Board this Ship, and he is almost a head taller than Brother Charles. . . . I hear there is 80,000 dollars on Board the *Ville de Paris*, which I believe is the truth.

The writer, in time, rose to flag rank himself. The process would certainly not have been hindered by the fact that an aunt of his had married Admiral Lord Anson, since for many years to come influence would be important, often vital, in reaching the rank of post captain and thus, in course of strict seniority, that of admiral.

Rodney's feat of arms enabled Britain to make a better peace than she might otherwise have done, and it marked the end of a stark period for the Navy. It was also the last occasion when there would be a certain atmosphere of chivalry between French and British at sea: the navy represented by de Grasse and Suffren was soon to disintegrate in the course of a revolution which would convulse Europe during the decade following the important battle off Dominica. When the French navy was reformed, it fought in quite a different spirit, guided by representatives of the Revolution – political officials who ensured that officers and men did their duty. With the Spanish it was different, and the spirit of chivalry was never entirely lost.

The captains of the War of American Independence became the admirals of the next conflict. They included Cornwallis, who had commanded the *Canada* of seventy-four guns under Rodney and who was later to have charge of Britain's principal fleet. Saumarez was to make a name for himself in the Baltic and elsewhere. Nelson and Collingwood, already close friends, had served against the Spanish in Nicaragua. For once there was a host of men of talent, accustomed to endure hardship, setback and disappointment, who would in due course bring the sailing Navy to its highest peak of attainment.

These men had seen the Navy stretched to almost impossible limits; served by dockyards in which corruption and conservatism seemed endemic; schooled in standing tactical instructions which with every successive generation seemed more constrictive. They faced French ships of excellent design, and an enemy who could rely upon adequate naval supplies, with morale higher than it had ever been. Even so, there had been few instances where French admirals, with the notable exception of Suffren, had shown any marked spirit of aggression. Their aim had not been first and foremost the defeat of the British fleet, rather the attainment of whatever 'ultimate object' the fleet might be at sea to effect. Sometimes, as at the Chesapeake, success attended them. Almost as often, as in the attempts to force the surrender of Gibraltar, it was thwarted.

Chapter Six

THE LONG STRUGGLE WITH FRANCE

For seasoned officers, there was at best a brief respite before the next clash with France, and in 1790 came a threat of war with Spain. This arose from incidents at sea off what is now Vancouver Island, where Spain claimed rights which were disputed both by Britain and Russia. A fleet was mobilized, giving many officers, who were at the time on half-pay, the chance of activity. In the upshot, Spain climbed down by admitting the right of settlement in the area of dispute. This was an important concession, increasingly so when the western parts of North America began to be developed.

There were some who saw in what was known as the 'Spanish Armament' a waste of public money. In fact, the crisis proved of use. When war began again in earnest three years later, partly as the result of the occupation of the Netherlands by the French Revolutionary armies and the consequent threat to English trade with the Continent and elsewhere, the Navy was more prepared than it had been on many earlier occasions. There were, moreover, two veterans clearly fitted for high command. One was Howe, who – as First Lord of the Admiralty – played a key role in keeping up the Navy budget before war broke out, the other Samuel Hood, whose younger brother Alexander was also high on the list of flag-officers.

In the case of Howe, a leading spirit in three separate wars, trust was certainly not misplaced, and the King himself never felt quite at ease unless his favourite Admiral was at the head of his principal fleet. Howe himself, a realist if ever there was one, considered that at sixty a man was too old for operational service. He was sixty-six and went to sea again only at George III's urgent plea. Hood, who was actually still older, had no worries on the score of age. Modesty was not something for which he was noted.

In the immediate future, Howe was to command in home waters, with the privilege of flying the Union flag at the main-top of his flagship, the *Queen Charlotte*. This was in recognition of the fact that he had held every important post in the naval hierarchy. Hood

The *Queen Charlotte* at the Spithead review, 1790.

was sent to the Mediterranean, among his captains being Horatio Nelson, who was given the *Agamemnon* of sixty-four guns. For a ship of the line, the *Agamemnon* was small, but Nelson intended to make his name in her.

The naval campaign opened slowly, with no large-scale fleet action during the first year. There was, however, one significant encounter. On 20 October 1793, James Saumarez, in the frigate *Crescent*, captured the French *Réunion* of equal size after a two-hour fight in which the French suffered thirty-three fatal casualties and the British none.

Saumarez was knighted for this exploit, which took place off Cherbourg, close to the shores of France. It was important in indicating what Mahan, the great American naval historian, called that 'combat supremacy' which the British never lost, against the French and Spanish, during the entire twenty years of the struggle with Revolutionary and Napoleonic France (1793–1815).

In the summer of 1794 Howe, in a series of operations which culminated in a battle on what became known as the 'Glorious First of June', showed that what was true of individual captains was true of the fleet in general. In point of management, tactics, gunnery and seamanship, it was the superior of any opponent with which it was likely to be faced. There would be little of the sadness associated with the War of American Independence. The French suffered from the

turmoil of Revolution, while in Britain the administrative benefits brought by, for example, the work of Charles Middleton as Comptroller of the Navy (1778–90) were matched by a wide range of ability at sea.

The duel between the *Crescent* and the *Réunion*, October 1793.

Howe had a constellation of flag-officers with him that recalled the days of the old Dutch wars. Graves, of the Chesapeake action, was second-in-command; the others were Alexander Hood, who had been present at Quiberon, Bowyer, Caldwell and Gardner, all of them captains under Rodney, and Thomas Pasley. The Captain of the Fleet, Sir Roger Curtis, had been prominent ashore at the great siege of Gibraltar, though he was considered timid and ineffective by the more dashing officers.

The French Admiral, Villaret-Joyeuse, one of the lightning promotions caused by the Revolution, had on board his flagship, *La Montagne*, a man who was among the ablest political representatives, Jean-Bon Saint-André. The British had a rhyme about him:

> . . . he fled full soon
> At the First of June –
> But he bade the rest keep fighting!

This was harsh on Saint-André, but political men were, and indeed still are, superfluous in the day-to-day management of any fleet or army.

The victors of the 'Glorious First of June', 1794.

Villaret-Joyeuse had put to sea from Brest to cover grain ships from North America which were needed desperately in France, where the harvest had failed. He intercepted a British convoy and made some captures, before being sighted by Howe. The fleets met far out into the Atlantic: as the French had the windward position, it became Howe's task to secure it, or the enemy would be able to retire without a battle. He succeeded during an engagement on 29 May in which Villaret-Joyeuse was forced to run down in order to save some damaged ships, much as de Grasse had done off Dominica against Rodney.

Edward Codrington, a young Lieutenant on board the *Queen Charlotte*, who was one day to have chief command in the last considerable battle between sailing fleets, recorded of Howe, as he closed with the enemy:

> Addressing Sir Roger Curtis he said: 'And now, Sir, prepare the signal for close action.' Sir Roger said, 'My lord, there is no signal for close action.' 'No, Sir, but there is a signal for *closer* action, and I only want that to be made in case of captains not doing their duty.' He then said, turning to us by whom he was surrounded, and shutting the little signal-book he always carried about him, 'And now, gentlemen, no more books, no more signals. I look to you to do the duty of the *Queen*

Charlotte in engaging the French Admiral. I do not wish the ships to be bilge to bilge, but if you can lock the yard arms so much the better, the battle will be the sooner decided.'

The occasion indeed proved glorious, as George III was never tired of saying, though he noted in a letter to the Admiralty: 'one cannot help being mortified that probably the great convoy from America will arrive safely in France.' The 'probably' became a certainty when Admiral Montague, who had been assigned the task of interception, failed in his mission. Villaret-Joyeuse had lost seven ships, but he had not fought in vain. The French rightly considered that the price paid, tactically, for such a strategic success as they had gained, was well justified. Equally undisputed was the tonic to the British given by the sight of the prizes at Spithead. The King visited the fleet shortly after its return and presented Howe with a magnificent sword. Gold medals were also awarded, though in an invidious manner which caused more bitterness than pleasure among those who had fought well.

In the Mediterranean, Hood had the extraordinary experience of being admitted into Toulon by a Royalist party who were in the ascendant locally. If he had had enough troops available he might possibly have held it as an enclave, thus neutralizing France's greatest

Lord Howe on the quarterdeck of the *Queen Charlotte*, 1 June 1794.

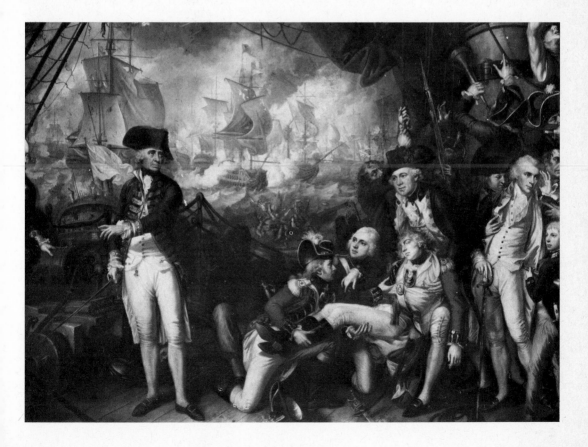

southern arsenal; but his adventure ended badly. The Revolutionaries, who had among their officers an exceptional young artillery commander, by name Napoleon Bonaparte, reacted strongly. Hood could not hold out ashore and was forced to withdraw his ships, leaving hundreds of Royalists to be slaughtered.

The destruction of the French men-of-war in the port was entrusted to Sir Sydney Smith, who made an indifferent job of it. Far too many vessels were left undamaged, or only slightly burnt. Originally, Hood had had some help from Spain, but the support was half-hearted and by 1795 the country had become an enemy. Spain was to change sides again during the course of the long struggle, and was not the only nation so to do.

Hood considered Corsica as a possible future base. The French garrisons were gradually expelled during the course of an amphibious campaign in which Nelson took a leading part; it was during the course of this that a wound cost him the sight of his right eye, though not the eye itself. After Hood had been recalled, his successors did little to distinguish themselves until the arrival of Sir John Jervis. This officer, a notable disciplinarian and fighter, had been well known to Wolfe and, like him, was a natural leader. In collaboration with General Grey, he had recently captured the French West Indian islands of Martinique and Guadeloupe. Jervis soon recognized the outstanding ability of Nelson and gave him an independent squadron with which to blockade the Italian coast. But naval strategy had to be related to events on land and the French were carrying all before them on the Continent; hence, in 1796, the British withdrew from the Mediterranean.

So badly was the war going that early in the following year newspapers spoke of 'the darkest hour in English history', as they had done before and have done since. Invasion seemed once again a likelihood and indeed it was attempted both in Wales and Ireland, though without any success. Commercial distress compelled the Bank of England to suspend cash payment in exchange for its notes, a practice it did not resume for over twenty years. Petitions were also coming in from the fleet for redress of grievances. Some were sent to Howe, who was ashore, others to the Admiralty. They were disregarded.

The country was treated to one gleam of splendour. This was the victory gained by Jervis over the Spaniards on St Valentine's Day, 14 February 1797. The Admiral was based on Lisbon, set on preventing the junction of any French and Spanish forces. The battle, fifteen British ships of the line against twenty-seven Spaniards, took place near Cape St Vincent, where Rodney had encountered de Langara seventeen years earlier. Jervis boldly sailed between two ill-ordered masses of the enemy and by superior gunnery and masterly manœuvres captured four ships without loss to his own squadron. Two of the prizes mounted 112 guns and were bigger than any ship then in the Royal Navy.

Opposite: Admiral Lord Hood.

The victory off Cape St Vincent. *Above:* the battle, 14 February 1797. *Opposite above:* Admiral Sir John Jervis, created Earl of St Vincent. *Opposite below:* Nelson receives the swords of the surrendering Spanish officers.

In this action Nelson, flying the pendant of a commodore in the *Captain*, wore out of the line on his own initiative, heading off ships which might otherwise have escaped. He captured two of them by boarding. Jervis gained an earldom, henceforward being known as Lord St Vincent. Nelson was promoted Rear-Admiral by seniority a few days after the battle, at the age of thirty-eight, and received the Knighthood of the Bath.

The news from Spain was welcome indeed, for during the course of the summer following the success there were two mutinies, one at Spithead, the other at the Nore.

The men of the lower deck, who fired the guns and went aloft and won battles, and who were generally referred to as 'the People', had every reason for unrest. Many of them were constrained to a life they loathed, enduring conditions which, even in a harder age than our own, were near intolerable. Their pay had been fixed at the time of the Commonwealth and they had had no increase for nearly 150 years. An able seaman 'received' 24s a month but the word is derisory: 6d was deducted for the Hospital at Greenwich, which few men – all being ruthlessly discharged when no longer needed – were fortunate enough to reach; 4d went to the chaplain (and clerics on board ship were regarded as apt to bring bad luck); 4d was earmarked for the surgeon, who often had very little skill. Even then, wages came in the form of a ticket which was generally cashed at far below its face value.

A seaman with a man-of-war's barge (*left*) and a 'master and commander' with a sloop of war (*right*), 1777.

The men were robbed by pursers; bullied by officers and petty officers; and received no pay when in hospital.

There was no regular uniform until the following century, but a list of 1663 of what were called 'slops' was not wholly outdated in 1797, and gives some idea of how 'the People' might be garbed. The prices did not alter greatly from generation to generation: 'Monmouth' caps of coarse yarn (2s 6d); red caps (1s 1d); yarn stockings (3s); 'blew' shirts (3s 6d); cotton waistcoats (3s); cotton drawers (3s); neats-leather shoes (3s 6d); 'blew' neckcloths (5d); canvas suits (5s); 'blew' suits (5s). By 1797 the 'blew' jacket usually had brass buttons and men often wore a tarpaulin hat.

The victualling was, officially: 1 lb of biscuit and 1 gallon of beer daily; 4 lb of salt beef and 2lb of pork weekly, with weekly rations of 2 pints of dried peas, 3 pints of oatmeal, $\frac{1}{2}$ lb of butter and 1 lb of cheese. This was the generous scale, but it was not often met. The biscuit, known as 'bread', was full of weevils; the beer turned sour after a short time at sea and the cheese was so hard that it could be carved into ornaments which kept their shape. There was grog, it is true, but men could be flogged for drunkenness, by which they escaped from misery into unreality. Desertion carried the death penalty in time of war, or a flogging round the fleet, which was a protracted agony few survived. There was no official leave given, though occasionally a rare, enlightened captain would allow this, running the risk of losing good men. Such generosity was seldom betrayed.

Samuel Johnson gave the view of most landsmen about the Navy, which he once observed as a privileged guest during a few days on board a man-of-war. 'No man', he said, 'will be a sailor who has contrivance enough to get himself into a jail; for being in a ship is being in a jail, with the chance of being drowned.' In 1759, the 'Year of Victories', his Negro servant, Francis Barber, thrilled at the exploits of the fleet, went off to sea as a volunteer. Johnson was so aghast for his future that he applied to Tobias Smollett, the novelist who had himself served as a ship's surgeon, to get him discharged, and this was done. Barber stayed ashore for good.

The men's grievances, among which inadequate pay and short commons were prominent, did not specify excessive punishment, though they suffered it in far too many ships. Horror is excited today by the idea of flogging with the terrible cat-o'-nine-tails, which a captain could order as a standard punishment. Some startling facts emerge from an examination of the punishment records in ships' logs. First, it appears to have been no deterrent; second, at least some of 'the People' of the eighteenth century were almost incredibly tough. For instance, in the *Victory*, which became Nelson's flagship during

'The Point of Honour': the captain and ship's company watching a flogging at the gratings with total lack of dismay.

the watch on Toulon later in the war, between January and July 1804 no fewer than 105 men were flogged, 13 of them more than once. One of them, John Welsh, was four times punished within this brief space of time: 10 January with 12 lashes; 5 March with 36 lashes; 5 April with 48 lashes; and 24 May with 48 lashes. In the light of this, the old word 'shell-back' for a sailor takes on a new meaning.

Welsh's offences were theft, drunkenness, more drunkenness, then more theft. Other common 'crimes' were 'insolence', which could mean anything, 'sleeping' (on watch), 'uncleanness', 'fighting', 'neglect' and 'disobedience'. It is true to say that even in a crack ship with a famous man on board, the lash was far too often applied, with far too little effect. Nelson's flag-captain, Hardy, was a stern man and the Admiral did not interfere with the running of the ship. On the other hand Collingwood, who was ten years older than Nelson, treated his captains as 'assistants' and sometimes actually referred to them as such. In later life he rarely sanctioned flogging and discipline was none the worse for it. One of his crew wrote later: 'a look of displeasure from him was as bad as a dozen at the gang-way from another man.'

The mutiny at Spithead subsided after the Admiralty had made panic concessions, granting a rise of 5s 6d a month. Howe redeemed his own neglect of notice of trouble by personally visiting every

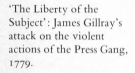

'The Liberty of the Subject': James Gillray's attack on the violent actions of the Press Gang, 1779.

The DELEGATES in COUNCIL or BEGGARS on HORSEBACK

ship involved. In his then state of health, the effort nearly killed him. At the Nore, Parker, the ringleader, was a professed agitator and the situation there was all the more serious because the men's chief grievances had by that time been considered. Order was restored with difficulty and later Parker, with twenty-eight other ringleaders, was hanged.

The mutiny at the Nore, 1797. 'Tell him we intend to be Masters', says the delegate with his 'Grog Can', in this establishment view of the affair.

The men involved had proved themselves to be the best sailors in the world, even when badly led. If well led, they were invincible, as was seen when Adam Duncan, with a scratch fleet, most of which had recently been mutinous, beat the Dutch off Camperdown in October 1797 and took eleven prizes. This was a pell-mell battle, with no science about it, like Hyde Parker's in the earlier war. Only one captain could be said to have done less than his duty. This was John Williamson of the *Agincourt* who had been criticized before when he might have saved Captain Cook's party had he shown more activity or courage in a crisis.

Lord St Vincent had a swift way with mutineers and with officers, admirals included, who did not meet his exacting standards. As a result, his fleet was so well ordered that when it was known that the French were preparing a great armament, destination unknown, under the

Nelson on the quarterdeck of the *Vanguard*, after being wounded in the head at the Battle of the Nile, 1 August 1798.

leadership of Bonaparte, he felt able to spare his best ships to re-enter the Mediterranean to seek out the enemy and destroy it. The chosen instrument was Nelson.

This officer had been forced to return home after an expedition against Santa Cruz in which he had hoped to emulate Blake, but where he had met with disaster, including the loss of his right arm. His recovery had been rapid and, once his health was restored, he sailed for Lisbon in the *Vanguard*. He was then sent forward on an independent mission, an order which could not have pleased him more. The First Lord concurred with the commander-in-chief that Nelson was the right choice, but the appointment caused jealousy among his seniors, one of whom was sent back to England.

Nelson's foray began so badly that it almost foundered. The *Vanguard* was damaged in a storm which dispersed the frigates. The flagship was saved by the efforts of Sir James Saumarez in the *Orion* and Captain Ball in the *Alexander*. Nelson and Saumarez were not close friends, less so than their wives; indeed there was an element of jealousy between two men who had rendered highly distinguished service and who would continue so to do. It cannot have helped the relationship that Saumarez had a hand in saving Nelson's ship, which had suffered through the inexperience of Berry, the flag-captain.

The storm was the worst trial, though a more protracted and frustrating one was to follow. Soon after his force of fourteen ships of the line and the brig *Mutine* were assembled, Nelson sailed for

Naples, expecting that, if anyone had news of the French, it would be Sir William Hamilton, the British Minister at the Court of the Two Sicilies.

Nothing was known for certain, but Malta was thought, correctly, to be a possible destination. Bonaparte had summoned the Knights of St John to surrender, which they had done by pre-arrangement; he had then left a garrison at Valetta under Vaubois and sailed on to Alexandria, with impressive ideas in his head of conquests in the East. Nelson followed him, but found the Egyptian port empty. Where were the French? Mystified and worried, he sailed back to Sicily. He had been too quick, and the sea too wide. The squadrons had crossed each others' tracks. And as there seemed nowhere else for Bonaparte to have gone, since his Oriental aspirations had become well known, Nelson returned to Egyptian waters. There, on 1 August 1798, he was rewarded by what was to him the finest sight in the world – the French fleet, embayed and at anchor.

The dusk and night action which ensued in Aboukir Bay was a masterpiece of valour and trust. Nelson attacked at once, giving the French no time to prepare. He encouraged the initiative of, and confided in, his captains, whom he called a 'Band of Brothers', as Henry V had done before Agincourt. The leading ship, the *Goliath* under Captain Foley, boldly steered inshore of the anchored enemy line. Others followed, including that of Sir James Saumarez. The French were 'doubled', with British each side of them. Their fleet of thirteen ships was destroyed as a fighting force; only two, in charge of Admiral Villeneuve, managed to weigh anchor and escape. The

Captain Foley, in the *Goliath*, steers round the head of the French line at the Battle of the Nile.

massive *L'Orient*, the French flagship, blew up in an explosion which was heard far away in Alexandria. Next morning Nelson, who had been wounded in the head, said that 'victory' was not a strong enough word to describe the scene. This was annihilation. Every captain, so Nelson told Howe, had done his duty. It was a measure of the quality of the Navy as known to the two admirals that nothing surprised Howe more than this: he had not always had such a happy experience.

Wounded as he was, Nelson did not overlook the wider scene, and this was characteristic of his genius. Having ordered Saumarez to convey the prizes to Gibraltar, he made two copies of his despatch, which he sent home by different routes – a wise policy, for one was captured. He also arranged for an officer to proceed to India; having served when young in the Far East, he knew the relief which would be afforded to the East India Company by the knowledge that a possible threat had been removed. Leaving a small force in Egyptian waters, later to be reinforced by Sir Sydney Smith, who distinguished himself against Bonaparte at Acre, Nelson sailed for Naples. He perceived in King Ferdinand III a possible ally in a new coalition against France. He mistook his man; but, strategically, the idea was not misguided.

Nelson's ships face the Danish fleet at the Battle of Copenhagen.

Misfortune followed. Nelson, whose wound proved to be more worrying than the surgeons had expected and left a scar on his forehead for life, came under the lasting spell of Lady Hamilton. King Ferdinand proved a bad soldier and within a few months was compelled to retire to Sicily, protected by Nelson's ships. Naples fell into French hands. Nelson returned there in 1799, Ferdinand joining him, and many rebels were executed. Meanwhile, Malta held out under Vaubois and when Nelson at last returned home, a peer of the realm and a Sicilian duke, it was to find his marriage ruined, and his reputation dimmed by the events in Italy. He was soon to enhance it.

The Northern Powers, Russia, Denmark, Sweden and Prussia, revived the idea of what was called an 'Armed Neutrality', aimed at preventing British interference with their trade. If Baltic navies were used by France against Britain, dangerous consequences would follow. A fleet was therefore organized to forestall any such possibility, command being entrusted to Sir Hyde Parker, a son of the Admiral who in 1781 had fought against the Dutch. He was a poor choice, but Lord St Vincent, who was then at the head of the Admiralty, sent Nelson as his second. Nelson persuaded Parker to give him charge of an assault on the Danish fleet at Copenhagen and in an action on 2 April

1801, which Nelson spoke of as the hardest of his life, the Danes were defeated. The feat would never have been accomplished had not Nelson put his blind eye to a signal made by Parker in the middle of the action, ordering him to disengage. It was sent just at the time when British gunnery was beginning to tell.

The attack on Copenhagen proved to have been unnecessary. Before it took place Tsar Paul I, the mainspring of the Armed Neutrality, was murdered by members of his entourage, though the facts did not become known until after the battle. Despite the news, Nelson thought that the Danes were likely to cause trouble later, and he was right. Their government remained loyal to French interests. In 1807 another and larger expedition was sent against them and Copenhagen was set on fire. The Danes lost much by their faith towards an ally, for when peace was made they lost their control of Norway in favour of their ancient rival, Sweden.

A single break in the protracted war occurred in 1802, when a peace of a sort was signed at Amiens, although many felt that it could not last Bonaparte had massed an army on the far side of the Channel and Nelson's last service, before he was given extended leave of absence, was to attack the invasion barges at Boulogne. He did not take command in person and the operation failed.

When war was resumed in 1803, nominally because Britain refused to give up possession of Malta, actually because Napoleon believed he was ready, Nelson was appointed commander-in-chief, Mediterranean, with his flag in the *Victory*, a ship which, though laid down as long before as the Seven Years War, had recently been rebuilt. Cornwallis was given charge of the Western Squadron, the principal home force. It was typical of Nelson's sense of responsibility that he transferred to a frigate, giving his old friend the use of the powerful three-decker until he had been reinforced, after which Cornwallis sent her on to her proper station.

Nelson did not step ashore from this ship for nearly two years. His duty was to keep watch over Toulon and to safeguard the considerable British trade in the Mediterranean. The watch was maintained by frigates, but they were sometimes driven off by stress of weather and twice the French fleet (led by Villeneuve) eluded them. The first time they were driven back by storm damage. The second occasion led to the campaign of Trafalgar and thus to the main action of the war.

The watch on Toulon provided Mahan with material for a vivid description. 'Those far distant, storm beaten ships, upon which the Grand Army never looked, stood between it and the dominion of the world.' The words were true, but the *Victory* herself, like certain other ships in a highly efficient fleet, was in one sense sharply divided. The Admiral and his staff, busy with tactical, strategical and administrative problems, were happily employed. The men, 'the People', who included many victims of the press-gang, crowded together with no chance of uninhibited relaxation. were punished

Opposite: Detail of Turner's painting of the *Victory*.

French frigates attack the
Arrow and the *Acheron*,
February 1805. The action
was a gallant defence of a
convoy by small escorts:
both ships were destroyed
but most of the
merchantmen escaped.

unmercifully. There were, in fact, two separate worlds within the stately vessel. They coalesced only in battle.

Before the main moves took place, Spain, which had enjoyed a rare spell of neutrality, ranged herself once again with France, though not for long. Napoleon's conduct towards the Spanish royal family, which he displaced, was intolerable. The alliance weakened and then dissolved, but not until after the Spanish fleet had suffered.

Also before the full campaign, there took place one of those fierce actions in defence of merchantmen, typical of so many in which small ships have distinguished themselves. HMS *Arrow*, sloop of war, and HMS *Acheron*, bomb-vessel, escorts of a valuable convoy, met with two large frigates from Villeneuve's fleet. In a four-hour fight between totally unequal forces, both escorts were put out of action and the *Arrow* was sunk, but their defence had saved by far the greater part of their charges.

Napoleon's scheme for the invasion of England was on the grandiose scale suited to his genius. The main French fleets were to emerge from Toulon and Brest, join forces with the Spaniards at Cartagena and Cadiz and sail for the West Indies, where they would be reinforced by a squadron from Rochefort. Once assembled, the huge armada would sweep back to Europe and dominate the Channel for long enough to allow the Grand Army to cross it. Napoleon believed that if he once got ashore in England, he would carry all before him and then dictate his own terms in London.

This was the plan of a soldier, as Napoleon would have realized if he had reconsidered the fate of his expedition to Egypt, when the army had been left like cut flowers in a vase and he had himself been lucky to return to France in a fast Venetian-built frigate. Villeneuve got away from Toulon and clear into the Atlantic, but no Spanish ships joined him from Cartagena. When he reached the West Indies

he surmised, accurately as it proved, that Cornwallis must have punched back the Brest ships the moment they were clear of harbour, for there was no sign of them, or of the Rochefort contingent.

Villeneuve, with his combined fleet of ships from the Mediterranean and Cadiz, was so apprehensive about Nelson, whose whereabouts he did not know, that he sailed for Europe prematurely. He was met by a squadron under Sir Rober Calder in July 1805 and two Spanish ships were captured. Later on, he put in to Cadiz, where he was watched by a small force under Collingwood.

Nelson chased Villeneuve, first in the direction ot Egypt and then, when he had gathered firmer news, to the Caribbean: the ocean being vast, he missed his quarry. He was in much inferior numbers to those of the combined fleet, though this never mattered to him. So certain did he feel of the superiority of his ships and men to those opposed to him that the question uppermost in his mind was not the possible danger to his country, which he thought was small, but how best he could destroy the enemy fleet.

After his return from the West Indies, Nelson had a short spell ashore and then sailed to reinforce Collingwood. Nelson himself believed that Villeneuve would come out, though some of his captains felt otherwise. In the upshot, the French Admiral's hand was forced by Napoleon, who struck his tents on the shores of the Channel and told Villeneuve to return to Toulon. To make sure that his orders were obeyed, the Emperor sent an officer to replace Villeneuve – in whom he had lost faith.

On the day of battle, 21 October 1805, Nelson had twenty-seven sail of the line with him, against thirty-three under Villeneuve. Nelson allowed the combined fleet to clear the port of Cadiz, keeping his main force well out of sight, and forming line only when he was quite sure that Villeneuve could not hope to avoid a fight. Villeneuve

The satirist's view of 'the Famous French Raft constructed . . . for the Invasion of England and intended to carry 30,000 men' reflected British faith in her Navy's defence against any threat.

113

Sir Edward Codrington on the forecastle of the *Orion* at Trafalgar.

tried hard to get back to Cadiz, in spite of his orders, but he was too late. The fleets engaged at about midday, in rather windless conditions, though with a swell from the west presaging a storm.

As the British slowly bore down on the combined fleet, in two irregular lines, one led by Nelson, the other by Collingwood, Nelson wrote the prayer which has since become famous. It emphasizes once again that his outlook extended far beyond the immediate present. To make certain that his thoughts were preserved, he wrote them out twice, a process he applied to the whole of his last diary.

> May the Great God whom I worship Grant to my Country and for the benefit of Europe in General a great and Glorious Victory, and may no misconduct in any one tarnish it, and May humanity after Victory be the predominant feature in the British fleet. For myself individually, I commit my Life to Him who made me, and may his blessing light upon my endeavours for Serving my Country faithfully, to Him I resign myself and the Just cause which is entrusted me to Defend –
>
> Amen, Amen, Amen.

Nelson's idea was to split the enemy fleet, not allowing one part to help the other. He packed his punch, placing three-deckers at the head of his own line. His tactics were unorthodox, bold and resoundingly successful. They resulted in the complete destruction of the

enemy fleet as a coherent force, in a repeat of the victory seven years earlier at Aboukir Bay. It was almost as final as the bullet, fired from the gallant French ship *Redoubtable*, which ended Nelson's life.

Joseph Conrad, one of the finest writers about the sea ever to use the English language, who knew the waters of Trafalgar as well as any seaman of his time may be given the final words on Nelson. 'Not the least glory of the Navy is that it understood Nelson. In a few short years he revolutionised not the strategy or tactics of sea warfare, but the very conception of victory itself. He brought heroism into the line of duty. Verily he is a terrible ancestor.'

Although there was never a remote possibility, after Trafalgar, that Britain would be invaded, the war itself had ten more years to run, and all the achievements of Wellington's army in the Peninsula were in the future. Napoleon once said, 'the Spanish ulcer killed me.' It was the Navy which supplied Wellington and enabled him to win his victories. Not a soldier could have reached Spain without control of the sea route, and the Spanish sailors who had fought with Villeneuve were soon engaged on behalf of the independence of their own country, against the threat of becoming a satellite of France.

There was still much that the French could do at sea. Small, fast squadrons could raid British traffic and so could privateers. The most successful of them, Robert Surcouf, said to Napoleon:

Sire, in your place I should burn all my ships of the line and never give battle to the British Fleet, or show fight to British cruising squadrons; but I should launch on every sea a multitude of frigates and light craft which would very soon annihilate the commerce of our rival and deliver her into our hands.

Although Surcouf was wildly optimistic about what a *guerre de course* might achieve, there was much in what he said. British trade did suffer – but it never came within measure of 'annihilation'. This was due to two facts; the first was the efficiency of the convoy and escort system, which, though strained at times, provided the best security for merchantmen; the second was the cover provided by a predominant fleet, which ensured the security of the principal overseas bases and was the nucleus round which the escort system was organized. Furthermore, two complete areas were controlled by British sea power, exercised by two exceptional men. After Nelson's death, Collingwood ruled the Mediterranean, until he wore himself out in 1810; Saumarez, with his flag in the *Victory*, was supreme in the Baltic where, during the ice-free months of the year, his ships were to be found off Gothenberg at the anchorage which the seamen called 'Wingo' (Vinga) Sound.

The recapture of the Cape of Good Hope from the Dutch, January 1806.

The flow of goods continued both from the Near East and from the northern countries; two islands in British possession, Malta and Heligoland, flourished, especially in post-Trafalgar days. Napoleon's

Far left: Admiral Lord Collingwood. *Left:* Sir James Saumarez.

so-called 'Berlin Decrees', which were intended to subject Britain to total suspension of overseas trade, proved impossible to implement; at one stage part of the Grand Army was equipped with English boots! Months after the French proclamation, Collingwood wrote home to ask, in derision, how it felt to be blockaded.

Still further afield, the British Navy made the most of the chances afforded by French domination of Holland to secure control of out-lying Dutch possessions. The Cape of Good Hope had been seized as early as 1795 by Admiral Keith in the name of the Prince of Orange, who was in exile. It reverted to Holland at the Peace of Amiens but was recaptured in 1806 by Sir Home Popham and by troops under Sir David Baird. Curaçao, in the Dutch West Indies, fell during the following year; Far Eastern territory, including Amboyna and Java, was in British hands by 1811.

In North America, what became known as the 'War of 1812' resulted largely from high-handed action on the part of the British in stopping American vessels and searching not only for contraband of war but for deserters, of which there were plenty. The Americans also much resented the British presence in Canada and considered that British aid to Indian resistance was checking their own expansion to the west. An attempt by the Americans upon Quebec failed, but they won a notable action in 1813 on Lake Erie. Moreover, their frigates, in particular the *Constitution*, which is preserved at Boston with the same care as the *Victory* at Portsmouth, had successes which were reminiscent of those of Paul Jones, their brilliant captain in the War of American Independence, who had defeated a British frigate in her own home waters. It was left to Sir Philip Broke of the *Shannon*, in his duel with the *Chesapeake*, to show what could be achieved by first-rate gunnery, assiduously practised.

By the end of the Napoleonic wars, the British Navy had no rival afloat and it had established a tradition of victory. The run-down was swift and necessary. In 1813 there were over 600 ships in commission, manned by 130,127 men. Immediately after the war, in 1815, most of the big ships were laid up and the crews dispersed, but there were three appendices to what had been an exhausting if glorious struggle.

The first of these occurred in 1816, when Lord Exmouth was sent to secure the release of Christian slaves held by the Dey of Algiers, his squadron being reinforced by six Dutch ships, a happy and successful re-conjunction of old rivals and friends at sea. The second lasted from 1824 to 1826, when a naval force was organized to help to repel an incursion into Indian territory by the King of Ava. In this campaign, for perhaps the first time in war, a steam-vessel was employed by the Navy. Her name was the *Diana* and she was hired in the name of the East India Company. She operated under the orders of Captain Frederick Marryat, soon to become the principal novelist of the sailing Navy.

The last fleet action wholly under sail took place at Navarino on 20 October 1827. There, a force of British, French and Russian ships, led by Sir Edward Codrington, destroyed a Turkish-Egyptian fleet and played a great part in securing Greek autonomy. Codrington, who was still well under sixty years of age and full of vigour and

Opposite above: the landing at Rangoon, 11 May 1824. *Opposite below:* the Battle of Navarino, 20 October 1827. *Below:* the boarding of the *Chesapeake* by officers and crew of the *Shannon*, 1 June 1813.

decision, had not only taken part as a young officer in Howe's battle of 1794, but had commanded the *Orion* at Trafalgar. The action seemed a fitting curtain to a great epoch of sea warfare.

Codrington was still alive when in 1842, after a naval war with China in which, following Marryat's successful experiment, steam was once again employed in a small way, a treaty was signed at Nanking with important consequences for the future. Canton, Amoy, Foochow, Ningpo and Shanghai were opened to trade; Hong Kong was ceded to Britain.

At the climax of the era of fighting sail, the Navy was still recognizably that of Anson. The way to commissioned rank was by the old route, known well to Pepys, of what was called 'Captain's Servant Entry', supplemented by Admiralty nominations, officially called 'Volunteers-per-Order' but popularly known as 'King's Letter Boys'. It is true that a Royal Naval Academy had been opened at Portsmouth as early as 1733, but it was never very successful, either as an institution or in its products, and it lasted for little more than a century.

Sail demanded such many-sided expertise, so it was held, that any theoretical knowledge required in addition to the practicalities could best be obtained on board. Ships of the higher ratings carried a schoolmaster, from whom such men as Nelson acquired an education which by any standard was respectable. What was nowhere taught was any theory of war. Admiralties and admirals worked out strategical problems *ad hoc*. As for tactics, there were time-hallowed 'Fighting Instructions' which laid down rules for the operational conduct of fleets, modified, in the case of more thoughtful commanders, by 'Additional Instructions' designed to explain their own particular ideas.

It is usual, and natural, to emphasize the complexities of latter-day sea warfare, but from a contemplation of HMS *Victory* in her dry-dock at Portsmouth, it is not difficult to grasp the extent of the technical skill necessary to manage, sail and fight her. She is of 2,162 tons burden; her extreme length is 226 feet 6 inches; her main-mast rises 208 feet above the water-line. When her three masts and bowsprit were crowded with canvas, it required nerve, muscle, co-ordination and deftness aloft if she were to show her full capabilities. Over a hundred men were necessary for the task.

Besides the carronades or short guns first produced in 1779 and considered by Bonaparte a winning weapon at close range, and other light guns on her quarter-deck and forecastle, the *Victory*'s three gun decks were alive with men. On the upper deck, where there were ranged 30 twelve-pounders, there were 150 of them. On the middle deck, to tend 28 twenty-four-pounders, were 168 men. On the lower deck, which supported the heaviest armament, 225 men tended 30 thirty-two-pounders, weighing over a ton. All these guns had to be loaded, cleaned and reloaded by hand, though a smart crew could complete the operation in ninety seconds, nearly twice

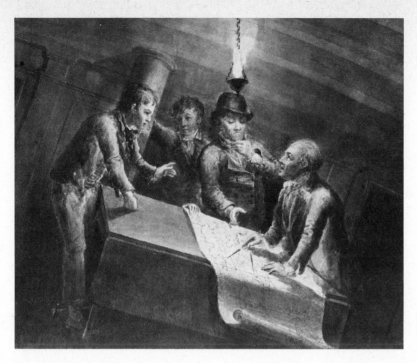

Midshipmen under
instruction in navigation at
the end of the eighteenth
century.

as fast as most of their opponents. A broadside was never simultaneous,
but a protracted ripple of fire. Apart from the difficulty of syn-
chronization, a simultaneous firing of so many guns would have
shattered the wooden structure of the ship.

All through the age of sail, finding men to serve the King's ships
was the great trouble. They could be knocked into shape, once on
board, by the older hands, but there were seldom enough, despite
Pitt's attempts to improve the situation through Quota Acts, requiring
large towns to supply a certain number of men. Almost any able-
bodied material was welcome. Two urgent letters from Nelson
himself illustrate this. When off Lisbon, on his way to Trafalgar, he
sent a message to the British Consul: 'I have to request that every
man who can be raised at Lisbon may be placed for the Fleet under
my command.' He wrote the same day to a frigate captain, then in
the Tagus, 'Get every man, in every way.' Men of many nationalities
fought with Nelson in his last battle.

The sailors lived on the particular gun deck which was their battle
station. They slept in hammocks slung between the deck beams.
These were only twenty inches apart, but as the crew was divided
into day and night watches, each man had forty inches to himself.
He ate with his messmates at a narrow table, hooked up when not
in use between the beams. He was allowed a gallon of beer a day to
wash down his beef or pork, which was so hard as to be almost
inedible at times, even after being boiled for hours. Instead of bread,
he had biscuit. A midshipman who was killed at Trafalgar once

wrote of this biscuit as 'making your throat cold owing to the maggots, which are very cold when you eat them . . . being very fat indeed'.

There are two statements about the sailing Navy which should give pause for thought. The first was made by Admiral Vernon in the eighteenth century. 'Our Fleets', he said, 'are defrauded by injustice, manned by violence, and maintained by cruelty.' Nearer our own time, John Masefield, who had himself served before the mast and later, as a scholar, had studied the logs of the great sea battles, concluded that 'our naval glory was built up by the blood and agony of thousands of barbarously maltreated men.' As in Disraeli's time, there were 'Two Worlds': the difference was not, on board ship, altogether between the Rich and the Poor, but between officers and 'People'.

Not a great many authentic records from the lower deck have survived to see print and scarcely any of them appeared when they might have had most effect – in their own time. Yet they do exist and sometimes they contain passages which must surely attract sympathy, as well as reinforce our knowledge of the difficulties of recruitment in the sailing Navy. For instance, William Richardson, whose narrative appeared just over a century after Trafalgar, wrote of those with whom he had served:

> People may talk of negro slavery and the whip, but let them look nearer home and see a poor sailor arrived from a long voyage, exulting in the pleasure of soon being among his dearest friends and relations. Behold him just entering the door when a press gang seizes him like a felon, drags him away and puts him in the tender's hold, and from thence he is sent on board a man-of-war perhaps ready to sail to some foreign station, without either seeing his wife, friends or relations; and if he complains, he is likely to be seized up and flogged with a cat, and if he deserts he is flogged round the fleet nearly to death. Surely they had better shoot a man at once: it would be greater lenity.

Chapter Seven

MANY INVENTIONS

If Nelson was an exemplar, he was also among the last of a race of admirals to whom had fallen the paramount duty of defeating rivals who could at least aspire to sea supremacy, even if they never achieved it. With the conclusion, in 1815, of the protracted struggle with Napoleon, the Navy took on a new role. The age of challenge had ended: that of expansion, exemplified in earlier days so notably by Cook and his immediate successors, would continue, along with the task of maintenance, the guardianship of what had been won. The stimulus provided by rivalry was lacking, and although the Navy could henceforward be used as an almost unfailing instrument of enlightened self-interest within the sphere of foreign policy, there was a danger that its once-eager spirit would atrophy. Nelson indeed became the patron saint of the service, but his qualities were too often disregarded. His especial virtue as a tactician had been that he treated every situation on its merits, acting accordingly, inhibited by no hallowed rules, disregarding tradition when necessary. He placed generous trust in his subordinates, and he allowed them such freedom of action that they not only did their best at all times under his leadership, but as often as not excelled themselves. As a result, his moral ascendancy over the enemy was complete, even before battle had been joined.

His influence was far less than it could have been. When Conrad said that one of the Navy's glories was that it understood Nelson, the observation could be applied only to the best of his contemporaries and to pupils such as Sir William Hoste, who won a miniature victory at Lissa in the Adriatic in 1811. Their opportunities were limited, largely through the very achievements of their master.

Nelson had always been the enemy of rigidity of mind. No unalterable doctrine could be derived from a study of his own exploits, but inflexibility and complacency were the mark of his heirs. It took another dynamic genius, Fisher, whose patron saint was Nelson, to overcome them, and that was a long way in the future.

Left: the Duke of Clarence, later to become King William IV, depicted by James Gillray as a rough sailor, 1795.

Right: model of the *Charlotte Dundas,* the first practical steam-boat, built by William Symington in 1802.

In the century between the achievements of Nelson and Fisher, however, technological change transformed the situation.

Steam was the trouble. Active young captains like Marryat and Lord Cochrane, who, after brilliant frigate service, was forced to lend his talents to foreign navies, might be eager to use it, but the resistance of senior admirals to change of any sort soon became a by-word. Their experience and seamanship would count for little if the centuries-old fleet of 'Wooden Walls' was to be revolutionized by mechanical power, of which they knew nothing, and the very idea of which seemed detestable. The famous 'Fighting *Téméraire*', which had been second to the *Victory* in Nelson's line at Trafalgar, was sold out of service in 1838. One of the finest of British painters, J. M. W. Turner, who had been among the first to board the *Victory* on her return to England in 1806, painted the *Téméraire* in tow by a black steam-tug as she went to her last berth. Far too many professional eyes lingered on the ghost-like ship. Few dwelt on the tug.

This state of affairs was natural enough, considering the slow development in wooden ships for purposes of war and the fact that they had served the country so well. But there were other problems too. The list of unemployed officers of all ranks grew longer and longer, and the age of admirals willing to serve afloat steadily increased. In 1827, when for a short time the Duke of Clarence, later to become King William IV, was Lord High Admiral – a post usually held in commission – he did many eccentric things; he had some deplorable fancies, such as changing uniform facings to red, though it is true that when he found gunnery neglected, he would have improved it had he been given the chance.

The peacetime business of the Navy, which included suppression of the slave-trade, fell mainly to the smaller ships, and when, in 1854, the Crimean War made it necessary to mobilize a fleet to fight a war against Russia, glaring weaknesses became evident. By that time, ships of the line had in many cases been equipped with auxiliary steam-engines, but those who tended them were a despised class and steam was used as seldom as possible. Smoke sullied the sacred decks.

Pluto captures the slave barque *Orion*, November 1859. The slave-trade was made illegal by Parliament in 1807 but it persisted long after.

Admiral Sir Charles Napier.

No better admiral could be found for the Baltic fleet than Sir Charles Napier, an explosive veteran of sixty-eight, rarely seen without a cigar. He had certain endearing traits and when much younger had been a staunch advocate of steam. Scepticism set in with old age, however, and he was once heard to exclaim: 'When a man's body begins to shake, the mind follows, and he is always the last to find it out!'

There was an acute shortage of men, the result of a run-down extending over many years and also the perennial unpopularity of the Navy, with its harsh discipline, poor pay and non-existent amenities. Indeed, the First Lord of the Admiralty actually suggested to Napier that volunteers might be recruited in Norway, during the course of a stately advance to the Åland Islands, at the entrance to the Gulf of Bothnia! In the event, no Scandinavians seemed eager to join the lower ranks of the Royal Navy, and this was scarcely surprising.

Napier's fleet, in co-operation with a French squadron, took the fortress of Bomarsund after an amphibious attack against feeble opposition. The Admiral was later superseded by Sir Richard Dundas, who, though a younger man, achieved even less. Dundas sailed for Sveaborg, on the coast of Finland, a place sometimes described as the 'Gibraltar of the North'. Fearing Russian mines, he contented himself with a distant bombardment. This was noisy and harmless,

and was enjoyed as a free spectacle by the local inhabitants. Further
along the coast, British guns caused some forest fires and destroyed
a valuable stock of pitch, which had been bought by the British
government and was awaiting shipment.

The naval operations in the area of the Black Sea were in themselves
unimportant, but at least the Navy provided security for the army
transports, which suffered only from the weather, not from the
enemy. In the Pacific, Rear-Admiral David Price, a character rarely
mentioned in naval histories, overwhelmed by the position of
responsibility in which he found himself, committed suicide before
getting into action. He was sixty-four and, like other admirals of the
period, had seen no fighting since his youth, which explains much.

The Crimean War did one good service to the Navy. By revealing
the full extent of the problem of manpower, which had recently
been under consideration, it enabled the Admiralty to implement a
regular scheme of seaman entry and to consider the question of
reserves. The methods of the press gang could be tolerated no longer;
neither could the lack of an authorized uniform for the lower deck.
On 30 January 1857 the Admiralty issued a circular prescribing the
following items, most of them based on what had been common,
though never specified, for a good many years: a blue cloth jacket
and trousers (which might be white); a white drill frock, with a blue

Mate Lucas wins the
Victoria Cross by throwing
a live shell overboard,
21 June 1854. The picture
of the Navy as a whole that
emerged from the Crimean
War was less encouraging.

127

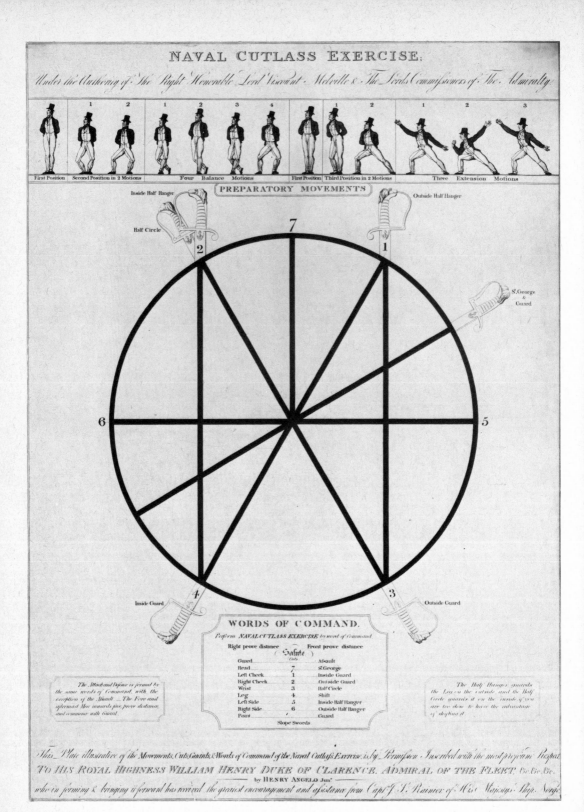

NAVAL CUTLASS EXERCISE.

Under the Authority of The Right Honorable Lord Viscount Melville & The Lords Commissioners of The Admiralty.

PREPARATORY MOVEMENTS

WORDS OF COMMAND.

Perform *NAVAL CUTLASS EXERCISE* by word of Command.

Right prove distance — Front prove distance

Salute

	Cuts	
Guard		Assault
Head	7	St George
Left Cheek	1	Inside Guard
Right Cheek	2	Outside Guard
Wrist	3	Half Circle
Leg	4	Shift
Left Side	5	Inside Half Hanger
Right Side	6	Outside Half Hanger
Point		Guard

Slope Swords

The Attack and Defence is formed by the same words of Command, with the exception of the Assault.— The Fore and aftermost Men inwards for, prove distance, and commence with Guard.

The Half Hanger guards the Leg on the outside, and the Half Circle quards it on the inside if you are too close to have the advantage of shifting it.

This Plate illustrative of the Movements, Cuts Guards & Words of Command of the Naval Cutlass Exercise is by Permission Inscribed with the most profound Respect. TO HIS ROYAL HIGHNESS WILLIAM HENRY DUKE OF CLARENCE, ADMIRAL OF THE FLEET &c &c &c.

by HENRY ANGELO Jun.r

who in forming & bringing it forward has received the greatest encouragement and assistance from Capt. J. S. Rainier of His Majestys Ship Serge.

collar on which were three rows of white tape (it is legend only that connects these with Nelson's victories); a blue serge frock, which became a blouse, tucked into the trousers; a pea jacket; a black silk scarf – again, nothing to do with Nelson's funeral; a black canvas hat with a crown, round which was a ribbon with the ship's name in gold letters; a working cap such as was worn by officers, but without a peak – alternatively, a wide straw hat. The circular was not always strictly obeyed and most men made their own clothes on board ship. There was indeed a regular bosun's call, 'Hands Make and Mend', Thursday afternoon being set aside for the purpose. This allowed for a certain independence, of which advantage was taken.

The year following the dress regulations, the Armstrong breech-loading gun was introduced experimentally, not with entire success. In principle, it was a reversion to the original ordnance carried in ships, which the muzzle-loader replaced in Tudor times. But it took two decades before breech-loaders became standard, in spite of the difficulty and danger presented to gun teams by muzzle-loading as the pieces grew ever larger. The last muzzle-loaders did not in fact disappear until the beginning of the present century, at which time pikes and tomahawks were still approved equipment. As if there was still a lively chance of hand-to-hand encounter between ships of the line, boarding and cutlass drill remained part of the regular training.

In an age when so much was being invented or improved, those responsible for the conduct of naval affairs continually looked over each other's shoulders, afraid of some startling development which would find them at a disadvantage. For instance, Anglo-French co-operation against Russia was still fresh when the French, who have always built fine ships, not only applied explosive shells to naval ordnance, but experimented in fitting armour which such projectiles rendered necessary.

The first sea-going armour-clad was the *Gloire*, which was launched in 1859, designed by Dupuy de Lôme. She was built of wood, but her vitals were protected by plating nearly five inches thick. The British replied with the *Warrior*, built of iron and with a speed of over 14 knots. She carried mixed armament, having 28 seven-inch smooth-bore muzzle-loaders, 2 smaller smooth-bore guns and 2 twenty-pounder breech-loaders.

Within two years of the appearance of the *Warrior* there was a weird and inconclusive duel between the improvised steam-frigate *Merrimac* and the specially constructed *Monitor*, the creation of John Ericsson, a Swede. The encounter took place at Hampton Roads, during the course of the American Civil War, and it engrossed the experts as the first operational meeting between armoured ships. It was difficult for any specific lessons to be drawn, except that for the future armour was essential, though it was clear that the design of iron-clads needed radical rethinking, including effective provision of big gun turrets. The events which took place in 1866 off Lissa, near the scene of Hoste's battle of 1811, added to the confusion. Austrian

Opposite: cutlass drill, demonstrated in this engraving of 1814, continued to be a feature of naval training long after it was likely to be of practical use.

The *Merrimac* and the *Monitor* at Hampton Roads, 1862.

and Italian ships engaged in a mêlée which seemed to suggest that, in spite of the improvement in the range of guns, the ram might prove important in naval warfare. This implied action at close quarters between large ships, a misleading and unrealistic conclusion.

More promising was the central battery, such as was mounted on the French *Océan* of 1868; but so uncertain were trends in design that a succession of ungainly vessels, of doubtful value, was built by the leading navies. The saddest instance was that of the *Captain*, designed by Captain Cowper Coles of the Royal Navy, which proved so unstable that she capsized in a squall, drowning her sponsor and most of those on board. The *Captain* had been fitted with sails as well as engines, as was then the rule. The first large man-of-war to depend solely on mechanical power was the *Devastation* of 1873. She had twin propellers, and four twelve-inch muzzle-loaders as her main armament. As she proved to be successful, she was an irritant to the large number of flag-officers who still insisted on the need for a full equipment of sails.

Especially important was the locomotive torpedo, the invention of an Englishman, Robert Whitehead, working at Fiume in association with Captain Luppis of the Austrian marine. In time, the torpedo, when allied with the submarine, was to prove the greatest threat the country ever had to face at sea. Although in 1870 the Admiralty paid £17,500 for the right to manufacture the weapon, it was viewed with great misgiving. Both France and Russia saw in the invention a potential menace to any surface navy. As a result, they ordered torpedoes for fitting in fast, handy torpedo-boat destroyers, which Britain also developed with great success and to the fullest extent.

It was at this stage, with destroyers growing larger and faster, that events seemed to crowd upon one another, causing perplexity and confusion of thought. The champions of the battleship, converted at last to steam, spurned the idea that such costly mastodons might become increasingly vulnerable to the lurking mine and to the torpedo fired under cover of darkness. Even so, gunnery, the battle-ships' chief business, was too often neglected in favour of brasswork and ceremonial, in spite of the work and example of such admirals as Sir Percy Scott, and of the fact that, ever since 1830, there had been a gunnery school at Portsmouth renowned for its standards and discipline.

The ill-fated *Captain* (*above*), with (*below*) a happier portent of technological progress: the *Devastation*.

Royal Naval College, Dartmouth, 1910.

It took a series of harsh jolts to bring the British Navy into a fuller realization of what might lie before it. Many of them were administered by Admiral Sir John Fisher, who took office as First Sea Lord in 1904, after years in important commands, when he had been a fruitful source of ideas for bringing the service not merely up to date, but well ahead of all rivals.

Fisher was known for ruthlessness, drive and humour. 'I am ready for the fray,' he once wrote to a friend. 'It will be a case of *Athanasius contra mundum*. Very sorry for Mundum, as Athanasius is going to win.' He won all right, but he left the Navy divided, with 'foes foaming in his wake', as Winston Churchill put it. Nevertheless, he renewed the service to which he was so wholeheartedly devoted in a way that only a genius could have done, starting from the bottom and working upwards at lightning speed. He had sponsored or encouraged various schemes of officer training to replace the antiquated or haphazard methods which had served earlier generations. He had hoped, for example, that executive and engineer officers might climb the same ladder of advancement by interchangeability, but it was asking too much to expect an officer to become an engineer for a number of years and then return to executive duties, and his idea came to nothing.

Regular training ships had been a feature since the mid-nineteenth century; the *Illustrious* dated from 1857, the *Britannia* from two years later. The *Britannia* burgeoned in Fisher's time into the Royal Naval College, Dartmouth – the splendour of its conception symbolized in the architectural aspirations of Sir Aston Webb. Engineers had their own ship, the *Marlborough*, by 1880, and later still their own college, at Manadon, Plymouth. For lower-deck entry, there was established in 1905 the *Ganges*, situated at Shotley on a spit of land known as Bloody Point, where the rivers Orwell and Stour join forces near Harwich. The *Ganges* was among the more noteworthy, though less publicized, of Fisher's varied achievements.

One of the ways in which world events helped Fisher was the alliance, from 1902 onwards, between Britain and Japan. This enabled him to concentrate upon a threat from Germany, which for the first time in history was building a major fleet and never concealed the direction in which one day it might be used. For Britain, this implied a contraction in world strategy, and a concentration of force in home waters not previously surpassed in time of peace. The principle of challenge once more became applicable.

The chief aim of the alliance with Japan was to maintain the *status quo* in the Far East and to keep the door open for trade with China. The Boxer Rising of 1900 gave the naval powers the chance to assess each others' strengths and weaknesses, for both ships and shore parties were actively engaged against the Chinese during the troubles. The Rising had not long been subdued when war broke out between Japan and Russia. The climax at sea came in 1905, when Admiral Togo annihilated his opponents at Tsushima. Certain lessons were confirmed for the British, who had built a large proportion of the Japanese fleet and had helped to train its officers and men. Effective gun range had risen to over fifteen thousand yards in the case of ordnance of the largest calibre: the way was clear for the *Dreadnought*, the first all big-gun turbine-driven battleship, a vessel which, at a stroke, rendered all previous construction obsolete. Although the *Dreadnought* was Fisher's creation, she was partly based on specifications proposed by Vittorio Cuniberti, the Italian designer, and she was approved by the greatest living authority on sea warfare, Alfred Mahan, who had hoped that his own nation, America, would lead the way.

Some idea of the speed at which the construction of the *Dreadnought* proceeded can be obtained from a series of dates. Her keel-plate was laid in Plymouth Dockyard on 2 October 1905. She was launched by King Edward VII on 10 February 1906. She did her sea trials on 3 October the same year and she was completed in December. This

The launch of the *Dreadnought*, 10 February 1906.

great ship, of twenty thousand tons displacement at full load, had a speed of over 21 knots and was armed with ten twelve-inch guns.

In his pursuit of hitting power, speed and simplification, Fisher added greatly to the efficiency of the Navy, though not all of his ideas were equally successful. Two years after the *Dreadnought* came the *Invincible*, the first battle-cruiser. The battle-cruiser, a hybrid, was less well armed and decidedly less well armoured than the battleship, although she was faster. The *Invincible*, built on the Tyne, was designed for 25–26 knots and carried eight twelve-inch guns, but had a six-inch armour belt, unlike the eleven-inch belt on the *Dreadnought*. She, and her sister ships, would have a chequered history.

Both the *Dreadnought* and the *Invincible* were followed by a succession of battleships and battle-cruisers, culminating in the Queen Elizabeth class, completed during the First World War. By general consent, these were the finest capital ships of their era. They did splendid service in two world wars, before the *Barham*, which had not been fully modernized, was sunk by a U-boat after half a century afloat, with the loss of all but 300 of her complement of 1,150. The class was oil-fired, but the *Queen Elizabeth* had a polished shovel mounted on her quarter-deck, inscribed 'Lest we Forget' – a reminder of the toil and grime of coaling ship, which remained general until the gradual change in the entire Navy to oil-firing was complete.

The battle-cruiser
Invincible.

Fisher was not unaware of the potential of the submarine, which, after a long period of gestation, became an ocean-going proposition with the appearance of the French *Narval* in 1899, designed by Maxime Laubeuf. At that time, Anglo-French relations were far from cordial, and it was to America that Britain turned when, at Fisher's insistence, she embarked on a submarine programme. The design chosen was that of John Holland. It had useful attributes, but lacked the double hull of the Laubeuf submarine, which gave full buoyancy when on the surface.

The Germans bided their time, entering the field somewhat later than other interested powers and profiting by experience abroad. When they obtained a lead in developments, they retained it. The marriage of submarine hull and Whitehead torpedo, which was to prove so lethal, had been accomplished as early as the 1880s by Torsten Nordenfelt, a Swede, one of whose vessels was actually present at the Jubilee Naval Review of Queen Victoria, held at Spithead in 1887. There, it was looked upon as a mildly interesting freak. Before long, the Germans were able to show what a trans-formation in sea warfare the submarine could bring about.

Fisher had been equally perceptive. As early as 1904 he wrote:

> It's astounding to me, *perfectly astounding*, how the very best amongst us absolutely fail to realise the vast impending revolution in naval war-fare and naval strategy that the submarine will accomplish. I have just written a paper on the subject, but it's so violent that I am keeping it! . . . I don't think it is even *faintly* realised – *the immense impending revolution which the submarines will effect as offensive weapons of war.*

Many admirals spoke scornfully of the early submarines as 'Fisher's toys', but there was a handful of young officers who were to prove his words true and show that, while the Germans might possess tech-nical advantages, even their foremost U-boat aces could show no finer record than their British equivalents, who had less opportunity to employ their skill.

The *Dreadnought* had stimulated a building race in naval armaments which nothing checked. In 1911 a young politician, Winston Churchill, then aged thirty-six, was given charge at the Admiralty, which Fisher, after an exceptionally long tenure as professional head of the Navy, had left the year before. Churchill continued in Fisher's dynamic tradition. With him, as his Naval Secretary, was Rear-Admiral Sir David Beatty. Beatty had been given flag rank at the age of thirty-nine, the youngest promotion since the time of Nelson, resulting from a fighting record in the Sudan and in China. He was forty-one at the time of his Admiralty appointment and his ways suited those of Churchill admirably. Shortly before the war of 1914 Beatty was given command of the battle-cruisers, and the Grand Fleet (the name given to the principal sea command in home waters), which then comprised the largest naval concentration in the world, prepared to face the challenge from across the North Sea, called 'The German Ocean' by the ineffable Kaiser.

The general belief was that the fleet was second to none as a fighting service. The men who composed it were better treated in every respect than their predecessors and far better trained. By contemporary standards, pay was tolerable; leave was provided for; and punishments were no longer so archaic. In 1871 flogging had been 'suspended in peacetime', though it was eight years before it was 'suspended in wartime', and ten before the Army gave it up. This particular brutality lingered in the gun-room, where midshipmen, known as 'warts', no doubt to give them a proper idea of the dignity of their profession, were beaten at the whim of the sub-lieutenant in charge. Conditions were described by Charles Morgan, who had served in the fleet, in a novel which naval officers did their best to suppress. Half a century later, Morgan's description was confirmed in every detail in the autobiography of a survivor, G. W. G. Simpson, who rose to flag rank.

Petty tyranny could be one of the penalties of life in the big ships, which were often less happy than smaller ones, in which initiative was essential and discipline less rigid. This was especially so in destroyers, still more so in submarines – and truest of all in aviation, which by about 1912 was becoming recognized as a possible adjunct to the reconnaissance work performed by cruisers, as well as being a potential means of offensive, once effective bombs and bomb-sights had been developed. In this sphere, the Germans, with their monster Zeppelin airships, were considered to have a lead. To some extent this was true, though the aeroplane proved to be of more value to the sailor than the airship.

A Royal Naval Air Service was formally inaugurated on 1 July 1914, a month before the outbreak of war. It contained a nucleus of officers who had already learnt to fly. The components of undersea, surface and airpower were therefore all in existence at the time of the conflagration. It was not long before the hitherto unchallenged supremacy of the surface vessel was badly shaken.

Chapter Eight

THE FIRST WORLD WAR

Britain's principal allies in 1914 were France and Russia, and an under-standing had been reached with France which involved a continental strategy, to the extent that an Expeditionary Force would be engaged from the outset on foreign soil. So far as the Navy was concerned, this imposed an additional burden on the many which would fall to it: the defence of the United Kingdom; the safeguarding of the Empire's world trade; a distant blockade of Germany (since mines and geo-graphical facts did not permit a close one); and readiness to engage the main German 'High Seas' Fleet, as it was called, if the enemy should decide that a big-ship battle offered an opportunity to reduce British strength.

Strategically, the conflict did not differ greatly from many earlier wars with continental powers, although amphibious operations, often so successful in the eighteenth century, took a secondary place. The true area of decision, so far as fighting was concerned, came to stretch as an almost static line of trenches and fortifications from Swit-zerland to the coast of Flanders. After four years of carnage and dead-lock, the Germans at last began to collapse and the renewal of open warfare brought success by land. The pressure of sea power was exercised silently but with ever-increasing effect, until, as in the past, it became one of the chief instruments of victory.

The war began with the escape of the German battle-cruiser *Goeben* and the light cruiser *Breslau* into Turkish waters, an event which helped to bring Turkey into the war on the side of the Central Powers, Germany and Austria. This in turn led to a campaign at the Dardanelles, aimed at forcing Turkey out of the war and bringing aid to Russia. It proved a costly failure, mainly due to the effective sowing of minefields and the comparative powerlessness of ship-borne guns against strong shore positions. It led to the departure of Churchill from the Admiralty, since he had been the main advocate of the enterprise.

One of Churchill's wartime decisions had been to recall Fisher as First Sea Lord, but although Fisher had his customary dynamic effect

Right: Sir James Guthrie's sketch for a portrait of Sir Winston Churchill.

Far right: Augustus John's portrait of Admiral Lord Fisher.

on administration, he became unbalanced and expelled himself after making a series of quite unreasonable demands to the Cabinet. His chief claim to success was that he sent two battle-cruisers to the Falkland Islands, where they avenged the defeat of a weak squadron under Sir Christopher Cradock by Admiral von Spee. German ships had quickly disappeared from the wide oceans except for von Spee's which had been based on China. They gave a notable account of themselves before being destroyed.

Nearer home, while the Expeditionary Force was transported safely across the Channel and continued to be supplied and reinforced until it had grown into the largest army Britain had ever raised, there were other events of much significance. On 28 August 1914 a mêlée in the waters of Heligoland Bight was decided by the sudden intervention of Beatty's battle-cruisers. The moral impact of the victory was considerable, but the planning behind the engagement had been haphazard and jubilation was soon tempered by two events which proved how vulnerable ships were to underwater attack.

The first occurred on 22 September 1914 when the elderly cruisers *Aboukir*, *Hogue* and *Cressy* were torpedoed in the North Sea by U.9. All three ships sank with heavy loss of life, including a number of naval cadets. No ideas on counter-attack against submarines had been developed and the loss would have been less had not the *Hogue* and *Cressy* stopped to pick up survivors from the *Aboukir*, which was hit first. This was in the tradition of the sea, but new thinking was clearly necessary if ships were not to present sitting targets to U-boats.

Five weeks later, in Irish waters, a new battleship, the *Audacious*, struck a mine which had been sown by the armed merchant-cruiser *Berlin*. In spite of magnificent towing and other efforts from other ships, the *Audacious* sank, after an internal explosion, before she could be beached. The Admiralty kept the news out of the Press, though it became common knowledge in a very short time. The ship had been at gunnery practice and the solitary mine which caused her to sink had an explosive charge which did not exceed 160 lb. of gun-cotton. Much had to be learnt about protection.

In January 1915 the battle-cruisers were again in action, this time off the Dogger Bank, against a German force which had hoped to surprise and overwhelm local patrols known to be in the area. The Admiralty was forewarned by intercepted signals. Contact was made early on 24 January and the Germans raced for home. A chance of annihilation was missed through damage to Beatty's flagship, the *Lion*, and misinterpretation of the Admiral's intentions by his second-in-command. The oldest German ship present, the *Blücher*, was destroyed, but the rest were allowed to escape. Hits on the *Seydlitz*, which nearly led to her loss, resulted in better safety arrangements to protect the magazines, a measure from which the British could well have profited. This was to be shown in the only full-scale surface battle of the war – Jutland.

Jutland will continue to be discussed as long as interest remains in naval warfare. It had elements of drama, surprise and disappointment. The German commander-in-chief, Scheer, hoped to trap an important part of the Grand Fleet, as the result of a foray by Admiral von Hipper's battle-cruisers. The British were sensitive about the effects of tip-and-run bombardments of the coast, which had occurred from time to time, and squadrons of cruisers and battle-cruisers were frequently at sea to prevent them. Scheer wanted the battle-cruiser forces to engage; then the High Seas Fleet would appear in full strength to settle the business. If the Grand Fleet were to come out

The battleship *Audacious* sinking, October 1914.

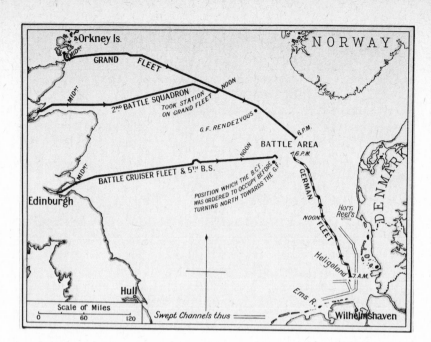

The approach of the German and British fleets at the Battle of Jutland, 31 May 1916.

in support, Zeppelin reconnaissance would ensure that U-boats were well placed to cause it serious loss.

Weather conditions prevented the original plan from being realized, but Beatty's battle-cruisers were encountered off the coast of Jutland on 31 May 1916, and an action began in which the battle-cruisers on each side were fiercely engaged, together with their supporting flotillas. By chance, Beatty had four 'Queen Elizabeth' battleships in support of him, but faulty signalling (as at the Dogger Bank action) led to their intervention at a needlessly late stage; Beatty lost two of his ships, the *Queen Mary* and *Indefatigable*, to magazine explosions. The *Lion* nearly went the same way and was only saved by the dying action of a Major of Marines, who ordered the magazines of the turret, which had been hit, to be flooded.

So far, so bad: but skilful cruiser work enabled Beatty to become aware of the presence of Scheer and his fleet, and he was able to draw the unsuspecting Germans towards his own commander-in-chief, who was racing down from Scapa Flow as the result of another signal intercepted by the Admiralty. Soon, within the confined area of the North Sea, no fewer than 148 British and 99 German ships of various kinds, funnels belching black smoke, were engaged in a battle during the course of which Scheer twice extricated himself from destruction by means of a manœuvre, the 'battle-turn-about' (*Gefechtkehrtwendung*), in which the big ships reversed course simultaneously. Only the Germans had practised this manœuvre and it was executed in masterly fashion.

When night fell, with the fleets no longer in immediate contact, Jellicoe felt confident of engaging Scheer next day and turning the occasion into another 'Glorious First of June'. It was not to be. Lack of reports, insufficient initiative on the part of the captains of the battleships, and failure on the part of the Admiralty to relay certain vital messages which had been intercepted – all these prevented success. Scheer was allowed to escape, having inflicted far more damage than he had received. He lost a battleship, a battle-cruiser, four cruisers and five destroyers. The British lost three battle-cruisers (including the *Invincible* which was with Jellicoe), three cruisers and eight destroyers. The difference in fatal casualties speaks for itself: British, 6,097; German, 2,551.

The moral shock resulting from Jutland was considerable. The communiqués from the Admiralty were unsatisfactory – Churchill was no longer there – and the British public, shaken by the dreadful casualties on the Western Front, and expecting another Trafalgar, had to accept the fact that the Navy had at last encountered an opponent equally skilled, equally well led, and in some respects better trained and equipped – and had come off worst. Some even spoke of Jutland as a defeat and the Kaiser, understandably, showered decorations on his fleet.

Yet the strategic effect of the battle was summed up in twelve words by an American journalist: 'The German Fleet has assaulted its jailer

The loss of the battle-cruiser *Queen Mary* at Jutland.

but is still in jail.' Jutland changed nothing. After the funnel smoke had dispersed, Germany remained blockaded and Admiral Jellicoe, who in Churchill's words was 'the only man on either side who could lose the war in an afternoon', maintained surface supremacy. Jutland was the last great set-piece engagement fought by the Navy.

The crisis of the sea war came after Jutland. The Germans had quickly discovered the skill of their U-boat commanders against men-of-war; merchantmen were still easier victims. There had been a great outcry in America when, on 7 May 1915, the U.20 had sunk the liner *Lusitania* in the Irish Sea with the loss of 1,198 lives, including 128 Americans, and unrestricted submarine warfare had been forbidden by the German authorities. When it was resumed, it had the most serious consequences.

By the early months of 1917, the whole British war effort faced atrophy through the effect on merchant shipping of submarine attack. There seemed no answer, since no one in authority had read

The U.35 torpedoes a merchant ship in the Mediterranean, April 1917.

A British naval airship
escorts a convoy during the
First World War.

enough naval history to realize that convoy was the secret of protection. When it was tried, it met with immediate success. Hitherto, the efforts of independent ships and patrols had been negligible and wasteful. It was only belatedly seen that convoy protection was the defensive half of the solution. The offensive half consisted of escort groups working not on their own but in close touch with the convoys, which attracted the U-boats, and round which they could be defeated. Within months, the problem was mastered. As the United States had entered the war as an ally, victory became certain, in spite of the collapse of Russia in 1917.

The German High Seas Fleet made more than one abortive sortie after Jutland, but many of the best of its younger officers had transferred to the submarine arm and a spirit of mutiny spread among the big ships, particularly after the advent of revolution in Moscow. The Royal Navy, now very much on the ascendant, mounted an attack on Zeebrugge on St George's Day 1918, in order to try to block at least one of the submarine bases. It was gallantly executed, though its practical effects were disappointing.

The war ended with the main proportion of the German surface fleet steaming to Scapa Flow to surrender – eleven battleships, five battle-cruisers, eight cruisers and fifty destroyers. This was an inglorious end and when the ships were scuttled the following year,

1919, by their crews, it seemed sadly appropriate. An Admiralty signal struck the right note when it stated: 'the surrender of the German Fleet, accomplished without shock of battle, will remain for all time the example of the wonderful silence and sureness with which sea power attains its ends'.

The cost was enormous. In just over four years the staggering total of 4,837 Allied merchantmen had gone to the bottom. The tonnage represented was 11,135,000; of that amount, by far the greater proportion had fallen to the submarine and the mine.

High tribute is due to the Royal Navy for its achievements between 1914 and 1918, disappointing as its performance sometimes appeared to a public that expected so much. It fulfilled its duties, even if it did not always cover itself with glory and even if sound thought did not always lie behind its employment. Officers and men upheld their age-long tradition of courage in the face of adversity – and the way in which the seafaring population continued to sail the merchant ships during the darkest phases of the war, with none of the publicity which was given to the armed forces, was beyond praise.

The British submariners are sometimes forgotten. Their most remarkable exploits took place in the confined waters of the Heligoland Bight, the Sea of Marmora and the Baltic, into which they had to penetrate against every kind of opposition. The task of the German U-boats was by comparison simple, with worthwhile and generally easy targets found almost everywhere they went.

The busts of the leading admirals, Jellicoe and Beatty, placed in Trafalgar Square long after the Armistice, reflect their stature. Jellicoe, who from 1914 to 1917 bore the burden of command of the Grand Fleet, was a quiet and modest man, of the highest professional attainments, who inspired the utmost loyalty in subordinates of all ranks and lived to become a greatly loved Governor of New Zealand.

Beatty, with the dash and vigour which belong to youth, with an Irish background, a love of hunting and a cool brain, was well fitted to the battle-cruiser force, which he led with distinction, though he was not always well served. He took over the Grand Fleet when Jellicoe became First Sea Lord, and it fell to him, for some years after the war, and at a particularly difficult time, to champion the cause of the British Navy at the conference table.

Jellicoe's stay in Whitehall was brief. He had become a tired man and it was not long before his period of command, more especially his handling of the fleet at Jutland, became the subject of controversy. A 'Jellicoe versus Beatty' paper warfare recalled the divisions prevalent in the eighteenth century at the time of the war with America.

The final words on a distasteful subject may surely be given to Professor Arthur Marder, the most perceptive student of the Royal Navy, from overseas, since Mahan. The dedication to the third (Jutland) volume of his history of events from the *Dreadnought* to Scapa Flow reads: 'To the memory of two distinguished Admirals, upholders of a proud tradition – Lords Jellicoe and Beatty.'

Admirals Jellicoe (*far left*) and Beatty.

Immediately after the war, during which 389 major vessels of various classes were in commission, manned by close upon 150,000 officers and men, the axe was ruthlessly applied and many able people left the service, which was drastically reduced. There was still much to do. For example, over a period of thirteen months a force operated in the Baltic, where Germans, Red and White Russians, and nationalists of varied hue, strove for mastery in land areas which had constantly changed hands since the Middle Ages. Finland won independence from Russia and so did three small Baltic States, Estonia, Latvia and Lithuania. They owed their freedom in the first instance to a British naval presence, holding the ring and preventing interference from the Russian fleet.

Losses were not light. Seventeen ships were sunk during this northern foray; also destroyed were thirty-seven aircraft of the Royal Air Force, which, since 1918, had absorbed the Royal Naval Air Service and its army counterpart. Over sixty other ships were damaged, largely by mines or from grounding in confined waters. Of those who saw Baltic service, two men were to achieve much in the future: Max Horton, who, as a submariner, had made a great name for himself in northern seas during the course of the war itself; and Andrew Cunningham, well known as a destroyer officer. Further south, the British Navy, in the Black Sea and in the eastern Mediterranean, had an important influence during the aftermath of war in helping to settle problems created by the Russian Revolution and the decline of Turkey.

The post-war interval of just over twenty years was largely conditioned, for the Navy, by the Washington Conference of 1921–22: there, Britain, which until 1914 had aimed at maintaining superiority over any two navies likely to be opposed to her, accepted parity

Air power: the new
dimension in sea warfare.
Here HMS *Furious* is seen
with her complement of
Sopwith 'Camels'.

with the United States; she also did not renew her alliance with Japan.
In any case, a two-power standard had been made impossible even
before the First World War by the rate at which Germany had built
up her fleet.

The ratio of strength agreed at Washington was 5:5:3 in respect
of Great Britain, the United States and Japan. France and Italy accepted
1.75 on the same scale. It was also agreed to limit the size of capital
ships; indeed, apart from modernizations, work on battleships ceased
in Britain until the eve of the Second World War, except for two
ships, the *Rodney* and the *Nelson*, which were redesigned to conform
with obligations entered into at the Conference. Britain was to face
the future with ageing naval tonnage, much of it of an increasingly
limited value. As the country was far poorer, in comparison with her
status before 1914, it was difficult to avoid this.

Victory, as so often in the past, brought its blindnesses. Senior naval
officers had been conditioned to the battleship and the big gun. They
looked upon submarine warfare with the same distaste with which
their ancestors had viewed steam. They believed that they had the
measure of the underwater menace through a detection device called
the Asdic, which was to prove useless in surface attacks by submarines
by night. They chose irrelevant episodes of the First World War for
detailed study. Jutland was refought *ad nauseam* and no protracted

thought was given to the most efficient protection of merchant shipping. It is true that the principle of convoy was accepted, but how best it could be applied remained unanalysed, and the building of relatively cheap escort vessels did not absorb as high a proportion of the Naval Estimates as events of the First World War seemed to warrant.

The possibly revolutionary effect of air power was also left an open question, although the potential of the Fleet Air Arm was taken with due seriousness and in 1919 the workmanlike aircraft-carrier *Hermes* appeared, the first ship of her kind to be purpose-built from the keel upwards. The controversy which for a time raged in the United States, bombs versus battleships, was indeed followed with interest, but it was observed that although the advocates of air power seemed to have made their point to their own satisfaction, the United States continued to keep battleships in commission. The salient fact was that only actual experience under war conditions would decide the full effect of air power at sea. In the First World War, Britain had made use of seaplane-carriers on some scale, but their value had not proved considerable enough to warrant the rewriting of tactical manuals. At Jutland, for instance, the *Engadine*, the only seaplane-carrier with the fleet, had only managed to send off one aircraft, and that briefly; she was then used to tow home a damaged ship, while a Zeppelin, on the German side, had flown high above the scene of fighting, quite unaware of what was happening below.

Beatty was exceptional, in this as in other ways, in his views on new developments. In a speech made at the Mansion House as early as 1923 he prophesied as follows:

> The fleets of the future will be commanded by officers with as intimate knowledge of the air as of the gun and the submarine. . . . It may well be that in the future the Commander-in-Chief of a fleet with his staff may be quartered on board an aircraft carrier; during operations his Staff Officers being in the air, far in advance of the fleet, giving information which will enable him to dispose his forces to obtain strategic and tactical advantages which would culminate in great victory.

Planning for defence was for some years hamstrung by what was known as 'the Ten Year Rule' – the assumption that there would be no major war for at least a decade. The impetus to this view came from the foundation of the League of Nations with the express object of preventing war. The League's champions became disheartened by the fact that the United States was not a member, although their own President Wilson had been the chief promoter. Their gloom was deepened in 1932, when Japan invaded Manchukuo (Manchuria) and it became evident that no well-meaning international body could stop a determined power from fulfilling aggressive intentions. A year later, when Hitler took control of Germany, the signs became even plainer and the Ten Year Rule had to be abandoned.

In 1937 an Anglo-German naval agreement was signed: Germany
was permitted to build up to 35 per cent of Britain's naval strength
and was allowed parity in submarines if, in her view, her needs
required it. The provisions were highly instructive; German building would result in a fleet consisting only of new ships and Germany
had already produced a successful so-called 'pocket battleship', which
was ideal for raiding. If she were allowed to build a considerable
force of submarines, against whom were they likely to be used?
Russia was at that time a land power. France offered no serious threat
at sea and Italy would shortly become an ally.

In fact, during the inter-war years, when she had been forbidden
to build submarines, Germany had experimented clandestinely in
construction, mainly in Dutch and Finnish yards; it was evident that
the threat from under the seas, which had been so real between 1914
and 1918, was likely to recur. The old sea war would continue with
new management and more powerful equipment.

The slide towards the inevitable was swift. Italy made a bid for a
cheap empire in Africa. For a time she succeeded, since the League of
Nations could not enforce sanctions and the Italians felt able to defy
the British Navy, even though a British presence in Egypt meant that
their ships and supplies would have to pass through British-controlled
areas such as the Suez Canal. Japan invaded the Chinese mainland.
Hitler occupied Austria.

Britain and France bought a year's time at Munich in 1938, but
when Poland became the next victim marked down for liquidation,
there could only be one end. Britain and France had guaranteed
Polish independence, though they had no means of fulfilling their

obligations if the Germans, or Russians, or both together, attacked the country.

When, in the summer of 1939, the Germany of Hitler and the Russia of Stalin made a diplomatic deal, the fate of Poland, and of the small Baltic states, was sealed; so was the future war alignment. Britain and France would once more face Germany, but this time the Germans would have as friends, either active or well disposed, Italy, Spain, Japan and Russia. Hitler had aided the victorious side in the Spanish Civil War and gained useful experience in trying out his armaments. Everything seemed in favour of the dictators – and appearances did not deceive.

It is true that at sea Britain had preponderant strength, more so than in 1914, and with the French navy reasonably strong, the Admiralty could feel a certain reasoned confidence in the prospects for the future.

German U-boat bunker, Trondheim, Norway.

As before, an Expeditionary Force was landed in France without hindrance or loss and a distant blockade of Germany was imposed. Although the sinking of the liner *Athenia* in the Atlantic at the very outbreak of hostilities was a warning of what might come, an unjustified idea was prevalent that the Navy had the measure of the U-boat. On the other hand, surface supremacy was never in question and, as in the earlier conflict, German merchantmen were unable to sail except as blockade-runners accepting a high degree of risk. Yet if, at the outset, the position at sea was not unfavourable, particularly as Italy was not at first an active participant, all depended on how the war went on.

Chapter Nine

THE ULTIMATE TRIAL:
THE SECOND WORLD WAR

The First World War provided the severest trials and produced the heaviest casualties in the entire history of the British Army. For the Navy, the decisive test came with the Second World War, the result of strategical reverses on an unparalleled scale, which reflected the impact of air power on all aspects of warfare. In the first war, the Navy could call upon such a wealth of volunteers that it was able to provide a magnificent infantry division to serve ashore at the Dardanelles and in France. In the second war, its activities called upon nearly 800,000 officers and men, together with 74,000 in the Women's Royal Naval Service, which had first been established in 1917. The regular Navy was enlarged by the Royal Naval Reserve, consisting of officers with experience in the merchant fleets, and by the Royal Naval Volunteer Reserve, usually landsmen by calling.

Some idea of the scale of operations in which the Navy took part may be gained by comparing the official battle-honours approved by the Admiralty for the two wars. The total for the first war was only twelve, of which seven were in respect of individual battles or operations such as the Dogger Bank and Jutland, the remainder being 'area' awards such as 'Dardanelles 1915–1916' and 'Belgian Coast 1914–1918'. The total for the second was forty-nine, over four times the first war number and almost equally divided between area honours and those for particular operations. These honours were promulgated in a Fleet Order dated 1 October 1954, so as to allow ships to carry authenticated scrolls recording the services of former holders of the same name. The most battle-starred name in the Navy proved to be the *Warspite*, with twenty-five battle-honours, ranging from 'Cadiz 1596' to 'Biscay 1944'. Next came the *Orion*, present at actions from the 'Glorious First of June 1794' to 'South France 1944'. There were many others which closely approached the *Orion*'s total. In every case, a large proportion of the honours derived from the second war, illustrating the variety of tasks which the Navy had to master.

The signal which went out on the first day of hostilities, 'Winston is back', is said to have caused elation in the fleet. With Winston

Churchill in his old post as First Lord of the Admiralty, and with Sir Dudley Pound, a dedicated centralizer whose experience of war had been limited to service in a battleship at Jutland, as First Sea Lord, two characteristics could be expected: emphasis on the importance of the gun and the capital ship, and direct interference by the Admiralty with operational commanders. Both gun and battleship were in fact on the way out and the fuller burden of the war would fall upon smaller ships, on aircraft and their carriers – and, as always, on the merchant seamen.

Sir Winston Churchill's incomparable services to the country were given as Prime Minister, not as First Lord, an office which he held – for the second time – only until the collapse of France in 1940. In supreme office, there was no one living who could have matched him. His months at the Admiralty were useful chiefly in bringing him back into the centre of affairs, after a decade in the political wilderness: they simplified the elevation of this remarkable man to ultimate power. By the time that stage had been reached, the Navy could look back with satisfaction on certain tasks which had been accomplished, though it had been many centuries since it had faced so difficult a situation.

Alliance with France once more necessitated a continental strategy and the Navy ensured that the transportation of the Expeditionary Force across the Channel went without a hitch. Another matter from which satisfaction could be derived was the way in which the cruisers *Exeter*, *Ajax* and *Achilles*, meeting with the raiding battleship *Graf Spee* in South Atlantic waters in December 1939, had attacked and then shadowed this powerful vessel. The *Graf Spee* was driven to take refuge at Montevideo and she emerged only to blow herself up. The action had a postscript early the following year, when merchant seamen captured by the battleship were released by Captain Vian of the *Cossack* from the prison ship *Altmark*, which was making her way back to Germany through Norwegian territorial waters.

There were other, grimmer facts, especially a German mining campaign, which resulted in heavy losses, and the skill of a new generation of German U-boat commanders. As we have seen, the Donaldson liner *Athenia* had been torpedoed by the U.30 without warning in the Atlantic on the first day of the war, resulting in the loss of 112 lives, though responsibility was not admitted by the German government. Orders had in fact been disregarded and Hitler had no wish, at that time, to antagonize neutrals, in particular America. Far more significant feats than the sinking of an unarmed liner shortly became known. On 12 September 1939 the aircraft-carrier *Courageous* was sunk by the U.29 while herself hunting U-boats. Here was clear enough proof that anti-submarine operations would prove acutely difficult. Just over a month later, Günther Prien in U.47 sank the battleship *Royal Oak* in Scapa Flow and returned home to a hero's welcome. His was a professional achievement which, in retrospect, all may recognize.

The German avalanche began to gather momentum in the early months of 1940, when Hitler successfully invaded Denmark and Norway. Worse was to follow. In May, the German army overran Holland and Belgium, by-passed the French Maginot Line and caused the British Expeditionary Force to retreat to a perimeter round Dunkirk. In a marvel of swift improvisation, the Navy, supplemented by small vessels of any and every sort, managed to lift 308,888 British and French soldiers from the beaches. Britain then stood alone, with only the Navy and the Royal Air Force fully equipped to defend her. Naval and air losses had been severe during successive crises, and with the defeat of France, the Germans controlled a huge arc of coastline from the Arctic to the Bay of Biscay, as a base to assault the British Isles.

By winning the Battle of Britain, the Royal Air Force thwarted any immediate prospect of invasion; but the Atlantic lifeline, at all times important, became more vital than ever for survival. It was essential not only in sustaining the war economy, but because it was the only way by which reinforcements could be sent to the Middle East. There, forces under General Wavell won prodigious successes against the Italians, who had taken advantage of the French surrender to seek what they could acquire.

Italian superiority in the Mediterranean was, on paper, immense, but the British commander-in-chief, Admiral Sir Andrew Cunningham, at once took the offensive and achieved a series of victories with slender forces. Malta held out. The Italian fleet made hastily for base after a first brief encounter between the surface fleets. The Navy's Air Arm made fine use of specialist training by a raid on Taranto on 11 November 1940 which resulted in serious Italian losses. Four months later, off Cape Matapan, the enemy lost three heavy cruisers in a night action which bore the stamp of aggressive genius.

The reaction of the enemy was swift. Hitler sent the Luftwaffe to the help of the Italians, the first result being a concentrated attack on the new aircraft-carrier *Illustrious*. The ship survived, though gravely damaged, thanks to her armoured flight-deck, and she was patched up, despite continuous bombing, at Malta. A more protracted trial was endured by the Navy when the Germans supported an Italian army which had invaded Greece. They came in such strength that a British contingent which was helping the Greeks had to be withdrawn by sea under conditions of extreme difficulty. These were added to when the Germans captured Crete by airborne assault in May 1941. The result: a further withdrawal of troops by a fleet whose endurance and resources were already strained to the limit.

Opposite: an English convoy to Malta, photographed from the air by the Germans.

Below: the RAF helps in the evacuation of Greece.

Losses mounted daily, for the ships had to operate virtually without air cover. After three cruisers and six destroyers had been sunk, and two battleships, seven destroyers and over thirty transports and fleet auxiliaries severely damaged, Cunningham's staff suggested that enough had been done and that any troops remaining would have to surrender. Cunningham's reply was memorable. 'The Fleet will continue,' he said. 'It takes the Navy three years to build a ship. It would take three hundred to rebuild a tradition.' Cunningham did not intend that, in spite of losses which most admirals would have deemed intolerable, the faith of the troops in the Navy should be shaken.

At the time of the duel between the fleet and the Luftwaffe off Crete, Hitler sent the new battleship *Bismarck* into the Atlantic, accompanied by the heavy cruiser *Prinz Eugen*. After being shadowed by the cruisers *Norfolk* and *Suffolk*, the raiders were intercepted in far northern waters by the battle-cruiser *Hood* and the battleship *Prince of Wales*. The German gunnery was excellent and a salvo resulted in the loss of the *Hood* in the same tragic way in which three of her predecessors had been sunk at Jutland. Although the *Prince of Wales* was newly commissioned and her main armament was undergoing teething troubles, she was able to damage the *Bismarck*, causing loss of fuel, before herself having to fall back on the cruisers.

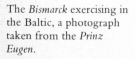

The *Bismarck* exercising in the Baltic, a photograph taken from the *Prinz Eugen*.

For a time, contact with the German force was lost, but it was resighted by an aircraft of Coastal Command. Shortly afterwards the enemy battleship came under air and surface attack, which led to

her destruction by the main fleet (under Admiral Tovey) then operating in home waters. The *Prinz Eugen* got away, though her supply ships were rounded up; it had taken the entire available resources of the Navy to bring the *Bismarck* to bay. No better instance could have been afforded of the disruptive power of well-handled German ships.

Admiral Cunningham's trials in the Mediterranean by no means ended with the loss of Crete. Supplies had somehow to be fought through to beleaguered Malta, the base from which British submarines maintained a continuous threat to Italian shipping supplying the Italian and German armies in North Africa – all this with a decimated fleet. The year 1941 ended with the temporary elimination of Cunningham's entire battle squadron. The *Barham* was torpedoed by the U.331; the flagship *Queen Elizabeth*, together with the *Valiant*, were badly damaged by Italian frogmen in Alexandria Harbour, although the fact was for some time concealed. The Italians were expert in such warfare, which they had conducted with some success against the Austrians in the First World War. They had attacked the cruiser *York* at Suda Bay, Crete, and put her out of action, though they were not alone in cultivating this daring form of the offensive: the British found it more difficult to decide on worthwhile targets, but for some months no part of the Italian coast which could be reached by submarine could be considered safe from similar operations carried out from Malta.

Hitler's assault on Russia in the summer of 1941 had afforded relief to Britain in the sense that the main effort of the Luftwaffe had been

HMS *Hood*: victim of the *Bismarck*. Only three survived from a total company of some fifteen hundred men.

A Russian tug helping a
ship's boat through ice
after the arrival of an
Arctic convoy

switched to distant targets, but it added to the burden of the Royal
Navy. The Russians asked for supplies and these could only reach
them by the Arctic route. This involved a long series of convoy
operations, doubly hazardous because of the proximity of German
air bases in Norway, and the certainty of adverse weather which
under the most peaceful conditions would not be contemplated with
serenity.

The convoys received no help and very little appreciation from the
Russians themselves. Losses were serious, both in men-of-war and
merchantmen. The climax came in July 1942 when convoy PQ17 was
ordered by the Admiralty to scatter, a measure which no one on the
spot would have recommended. It was one of several instances during
the war when the commanders concerned should have been left to
make their own decisions. The Admiralty feared the intervention of
heavy surface ships, including the new battleship *Tirpitz*, which was
known to be as formidable as the *Bismarck*. No surface attack of the
kind materialized and, over the months, the *Tirpitz* was kept inactive
in Norwegian waters. She was damaged first by midget submarines
and then by aircraft. In the end, she was sunk by the Royal Air Force,
having achieved nothing except alarm the Admiralty. PQ17 was the
victim of the Admiralty and out of thirty-six merchant ships which
sailed for Russia, only thirteen arrived. This was the worst loss,
materially and in morale, in the Arctic operations, which were in
general distinguished by great gallantry, particularly on the part of
the destroyer, aircraft-carrier and cruiser escorts.

After 7 December 1941, when the Japanese assaulted the American fleet base at Pearl Harbor, the struggle became truly world-wide. Britain sent two capital ships, the *Prince of Wales* and the *Repulse*, to Singapore, but no aircraft-carrier was available and they were sunk before they could play any effective part in the Far East. The loss was felt as a nation-wide shock, like the sinking of the *Hood*, but it is doubtful whether the dispatch of these important vessels could have had much more significance than that of a gesture, so stretched were resources at that time.

At first, the Japanese carried all before them: in the Philippines; at Hong Kong; at Singapore; and against the Dutch East Indies. Island groups were taken; Burma was invaded; India threatened; northern Australia raided. There seemed little to halt the onrush except perhaps the sheer scope of the task undertaken, which was to acquire the largest empire yet known to the Orient, disguised under the name of 'The Co-Prosperity Sphere'.

In the Atlantic, the Germans made the most of American reluctance to apply the lessons which had been learnt by the British in more than two years of endurance. Admiral Dönitz sent a number of his most successful submarine commanders to prey on unescorted shipping. They reaped a sensational harvest and they called the early months of 1942 their 'happy time'. The official name for their operations was *Paukenschlag* ('Roll of Drums'). For months the drums made a thunderous noise and attacks met negligible opposition.

The *Prince of Wales* leaving Singapore, 8 December 1941. Japanese aircraft were to sink both her and the battle-cruiser *Repulse* in a ninety-minute attack not long after.

American recovery, once under way, was swift. At Midway, in June 1942, the Japanese had their first serious check at sea; in the autumn Operation 'Torch' was organized as a first step towards gaining North Africa and thus acquiring the necessary bases for an invasion of southern Europe. The Germans were defeated on land at El Alamein and were held by the Russians at Stalingrad. Italy laid down her arms, thus hastening the ever-increasing use of the Mediterranean by Allied forces. France, under General de Gaulle, once more took an active role in various theatres of war, efforts which were to increase as liberation of territories hitherto occupied by the enemy grew nearer.

The British skill in Combined Operations, which had been so marked at the time of the Seven Years War, was revived under the direction of Admiral Mountbatten, who was later to be appointed Supreme Allied Commander in South-East Asia. Complete success attended a raid on Saint-Nazaire in March 1942, which put the largest dry-dock on the west coast of France out of commission. A few months later, however, when a sortie was made at Dieppe on a bigger scale, casualties were excessive in relation to the experience gained, chiefly because the key element of surprise was lacking.

In the Pacific, during the long and bitterly contested series of campaigns which were conducted by the Americans as they slowly

Dieppe: landing craft.

The *Prince of Wales* in happier days, meeting an Atlantic convoy.

fought their way towards the Japanese home islands, in many of which ships of the Royal and the Commonwealth Navies played their part, the United States' forces showed themselves to be masters of the amphibious assault, as well as of fleet operations. The campaigning was on a scale which dwarfed all previous struggles for maritime predominance. The aircraft-carrier became the capital ship, round which task forces were built.

The summer of 1943 was distinguished by a series of Anglo-American operations in the Mediterranean, to which Admiral Cunningham, after an interlude in Washington, returned as commander-in-chief. Sicily was captured. Landings were made at Salerno and Anzio; Malta was freed from the threat of starvation and resumed its function as a principal Allied base. In the autumn of that year, Cunningham succeeded Sir Dudley Pound as First Sea Lord and was thus one of the few commanders on either side who retained the confidence of the government he served for the entire span of the war.

Not many months before Cunningham transferred from his Mediterranean headquarters to the centre of affairs in Whitehall, Admiral Sir Max Horton took over command of the Western Approaches from Sir Percy Noble. From early days in the war, Horton had had over-all responsibility for the operation of British submariners. Now he was to be given the chance to win the critical Battle of the Atlantic, the only one, Churchill had said, that had him

worried. Horton was in a strong position *vis-à-vis* Dönitz. New equipment was coming in fast: more powerful escorts; more aircraft; better radar; ever-more sophisticated anti-submarine weapons. Radar was a battle-winning electrical apparatus, in which Britain had the lead. It enabled a 'scanner' to reflect objects at a distance, with immense effects on navigation and gunnery.

The battleship *Scharnhorst* (*opposite*, seen in the Arctic) was sunk by her British counterpart, the *Duke of York* (*above*) in December 1943.

Like Dönitz, Horton had great skill as a submariner, based on many years of experience at sea under war conditions. The duel between the two men proceeded relentlessly. By the middle of 1943, after a series of convoy actions in which U-boat losses became unacceptably high, Horton's task was achieved, though he never relaxed. Hunting-group commanders such as Captain F.J. Walker gained mastery over their opponents. Never again would the U-boat prove a supremely serious threat, even after the *schnorkel*, a device which enabled the Germans to charge their batteries almost entirely submerged, had gone into production.

A flag-officer who served with distinction under both Cunningham and Horton wrote of the former that he worked through 'humane discipline, vigilance, and an appeal to tradition', and of the latter that he worked through 'humane discipline, a most unusual knowledge of material and, on the spiritual side, vision'. 'This', he added, 'made for a nicely balanced expert performance by both officers.' These tributes could not be more succinct or to the point. By reason of his seniority, and of the paramountcy of his successive posts, it was Cunningham whose bust was chosen to be placed alongside those of Jellicoe and Beatty in Trafalgar Square; he was the only Admiral of the Second World War to be so honoured. Cunningham would have been the first to say that he stood there as the symbol of all fighting leaders.

Hitler's last attempt to make use of his larger surface ships took place in December 1943, when the battleship *Scharnhorst* was ordered to attack a convoy to Russia. A cruiser squadron under Admiral Burnett was in close support of the merchantmen. Burnett was able to counter preliminary moves by the *Scharnhorst*, whose salvoes did some damage to the *Norfolk*, though they did not put her out of action. The commander-in-chief, Home Fleet, Sir Bruce Fraser, was also at sea in the hope of intercepting the German vessel and this object was achieved on 26 December. The *Scharnhorst* was illuminated by starshell and sunk by the guns of the battleship *Duke of York*, following an attack by destroyers.

This was the last action between battleships in European waters. The engagement took place in darkness and no aircraft were involved. In a sense it was the end of an epoch: on the British side, no further battleships were completed except for the *Vanguard*, last of her breed. As for the Germans, the *Scharnhorst*'s end signalized Hitler's final disillusionment with his surface fleet. Except for the high-speed and aggressively used motor torpedo boats which waged ceaseless war in British, French, Belgian and Dutch coastal waters, the German ships, so well constructed and so heavily armed, had a poor record.

The supreme Anglo-American effort in Europe, designed to thrust into the heart of Germany, began on 6 June 1944 with Operation 'Neptune'. This was the code name for the assault on Normandy – successful beyond expectation, in spite of weather which was at first uncertain and which later did considerable damage to the artificial harbours created off-shore. Naval command was appropriately given to Sir Bertram Ramsey, who had been responsible for the arrangements for the withdrawal of the troops from the beaches of Dunkirk four years earlier. Tactical charge of the British forces was given to Rear-Admiral Sir Philip Vian, who, since the days of the *Cossack* and the *Altmark*, had attained flag rank and won a knighthood for fighting a convoy through to Malta in dark days in the Middle East, against the heaviest odds.

The forces afloat for the Normandy operations involved 125,000 officers and men. Some 5,000 ships, including 6 battleships, 23 cruisers, 104 destroyers, more than 4,000 landing craft of various kinds, with attendant minesweepers and auxiliaries, were present. Air cover was provided from bases in England. The Royal Marine contingent comprised five Commandos, an Armoured Support Group, an Engineer Commando and Obstruction Clearance Units. In addition, many of the assault landing-craft were manned by Marines, who provided their customary proportion of the complements of the larger men-of-war.

One of the stiffest tasks which fell to the Marines was at Walcharen, when it had become necessary to clear the approaches of the port of Antwerp, in order to ease the passage of supplies to the advancing army. This involved landing against severe opposition, even more so than at Normandy, and it was here that the veteran *Warspite*, in the

D-Day, June 1944: the landing of British troops, a proud yet curiously traditional scene at the dawn of the all-changing nuclear age.

The British fleet in action against the Japanese off Sumatra.

last duty in which she took part, covered the landing craft with gun-fire as they approached the beaches.

During the final phases of the struggle, the Navy was at last able to spare more adequate forces than heretofore, to help in regaining territory lost to the Japanese in the Far East. Sir Bruce Fraser commanded the principal British fleet in the area, the aircraft-carriers being in charge of Admiral Vian. The value of their armoured flight-decks, which had been the saving of the *Illustrious* earlier in the war, impressed the Americans when the Japanese resorted to suicide attacks by fighter aircraft.

With the dropping of atom bombs on Hiroshima and Nagasaki in the summer of 1945, acts which put an end to the war within days, scientists added a new dimension to destruction, under the shadow of which the whole world has since had to live.

The composition of the British Navy at the end of the conflict showed in a striking way the change in emphasis from the First World War, when over 70 battleships had been in commission. When de-commissioning began the list included not only 14 battleships, a few of them already earmarked for reserve, but 52 aircraft-carriers, 62 cruisers, 257 destroyers, 131 submarines and nearly 9,000 smaller vessels, ranging from frigates and corvettes to landing craft. More-over, the Fleet Air Arm operated 70 strike and fighter squadrons.

There had been a sinister similarity in shipping losses during the
two wars. Between 1939 and 1945, some 4,786 Allied vessels had
been sent to the bottom, but the aggregate in tonnage was nearly
twice that destroyed between 1914 and 1918. In the second war,
69 per cent had fallen victim to U–boats or mines, and 16 per cent to
air attack. Surface ships sunk only 7 per cent; of the remaining losses,
8 per cent were due to marine causes, the risks of which were much
enhanced by wartime conditions. Sensational as has been the record
of undersea salvage since 1918, the treasure which still remains
beneath the sea is beyond calculation. Thirty thousand merchant
seamen lost their lives so that their comrades in the fighting services,
and those at home, should be supplied.

The Second World War was won, after reverses on a scale never
before experienced, by the united efforts of the nation, supported in
the later stages by two tremendous allies, the United States and
Russia, who had been drawn into the conflict against their will and
by unprovoked aggression. The British Navy, together with the RAF,
had been the nation's principal means of defence throughout the
darkest years. The Navy continued to keep the nation supplied,
transported the army overseas to victory, and surmounted difficulties
and dangers in a way which few students of war would, at the outset
of hostilities, have believed possible.

British merchant convoy during the Second World War: would such scenes ever be repeated?

Chapter Ten

LATER EVENTS

Nearly six years of war developed the strength of the British Navy to an unprecedented extent. For a critical part of the struggle it was the only significant maritime force engaged against Germany and Italy. Later on the United States, with almost limitless resources, provided by far the greater proportion of the strength employed against Japan and took an increasing share of the burden elsewhere. The US Navy maintained its dominant position in the following decades, until Russia, awakening to the full possibilities of sea power, became a serious rival.

Britain could maintain third place among the leading naval powers only with difficulty, but when wartime losses had been made good, her mercantile marine once more grew to be among the largest in the world. For the future, the value of the Navy was seen to lie, to a far greater extent than ever before, in its contribution to alliances, an inevitable process as the Empire dissolved. Nevertheless, however small the Navy might become in relation to those of the super powers, there was no reason why, qualitatively, significant contributions could not be made, especially in the technical field.

Certainly the immediate post-war period indicated a continuingly active role, sometimes far afield. For instance, it was in Chinese waters, so often in the past a scene of activity, that an episode led to the award of an official battle-honour to the frigate *Amethyst*, which, earlier in her career, had taken part in the fight against the U-boats.

In April 1949 this ship was in the Yangtze River, her mission being to bring relief to the British Embassy at Nanking, when she came under heavy fire from Communist artillery and was forced to anchor. Attempts to relieve her failed and for more than three months the vessel remained in the river, subjected to spasmodic fire and recurrent threats.

Throughout the ordeal, Lieutenant-Commander Kerans had the fullest support from the Admiral commanding in the area, who signalled to him: 'I shall, of course, support your judgment.' Many a

The frigate *Amethyst*, showing artillery hits on her side, reaches Hong Kong, 8 August 1949.

man on the spot in time of past crisis would have welcomed such a message. In this case it resulted in Kerans deciding to make a dash for safety. The journey of 140 miles down-river was achieved at great risk but with complete success. Seventy-three officers and men were concerned, their average age only twenty-three. As if to balance matters, the ship was steered at the more critical stages by a Leading Seaman with twenty-four years experience afloat.

In the Korean War, which broke out the following year, supremacy at sea was at no time seriously challenged. The Navy supported the ground forces with gun-fire, with amphibious assaults which took the enemy by surprise and with carrier-borne air cover. Sixteen squadrons of the Fleet Air Arm were involved at one time or another, their precision bombing being spectacularly effective. After months of bitter fighting, the Communists were driven back beyond the 38th Parallel, the former boundary line between North and South Korea, an armistice being agreed in 1953. A total of seventy-six men-of-war from the navies of the Commonwealth took part in operations. Thirty-four of these, including four aircraft-carriers, were from the Royal Navy.

Throughout the history of the Navy, the achievement of military objectives could not be divorced from their political impact. When, in 1956, Britain and France decided to intervene in the Suez Canal dispute between Israel and Egypt, a task force was organized, including six British aircraft-carriers, to carry out an operation which would be wholly amphibious and airborne. Air opposition was soon eliminated and two Royal Marine Commandos landed from assault craft to seize a beach-head. Another Commando was flown in by helicopter, in the largest operation of its kind yet attempted. All the original objectives were attained, but a cease-fire was ordered as the result of world protest. Political controversy could not affect the point that the Suez operation reinforced: the need for mobile naval task

Opposite: HMS *Ocean* on its way to Korea from Japan, 21 July 1952.

Suez: casualties taken from a Royal Navy helicopter on board HMS *Eagle*, 11 November 1956.

forces which could be deployed at short notice to deal with limited crises. From this stemmed the idea of the Commando ship, equipped to carry an amphibious force strong enough to cope with localized trouble. Two light fleet aircraft-carriers were accordingly converted to accommodate a Marine Commando, with the necessary vehicles and assault craft, as well as helicopters. The first such ship took up her station at Singapore in 1960 and proved an immediate success.

Within a year, the value of these vessels was put to practical test. The ruler of Kuwait, threatened with annexation by a powerful neighbour, called for aid from Britain. Twenty-four hours later a Commando ship was on the spot and Marines were ready to take up positions along the borders of the territory until they could be relieved by conventional military forces. Again, in 1962, during the 'confrontation' of the State of Brunei by Indonesia, helicopter squadrons from the Commando ship *Albion* gave exceptional service; the biographer of General Sir Walter Walker (who was in charge in the area) declares that they took to jungle conditions 'with such skill, courage and zest that their feats had soon become legendary even in a place so bizarre as Borneo'. Fleet Air Arm Squadrons 845 and 846 operated from a forward base at Nanga Caat, flying with 'extraordinary dash'. The campaign was an admirable instance of Combined Operations – what Walker liked to call 'Jointmanship'.

The Commando carrier was certainly one of the most useful classes of ship ever devised by the Navy, but the two large fleet carriers, the *Ark Royal* and the *Eagle*, named after predecessors with notable service in the Second World War, were among the most impressive ships afloat, and their equipment matched their structure. In 1945 a British naval pilot had made the world's first deck landing with a jet aircraft. Following upon this, the Fleet Air Arm was given up-to-date jet fighters, and strike aircraft capable of carrying nuclear weapons.

Various inventions, which were also taken up by Britain's NATO allies, helped the new machines to be handled successfully. First was the angled flight-deck, to enable more than one aircraft to be operated simultaneously; second, the steam catapult to replace the more dangerous rocket booster for take-off; third, a mirror landing device to help deck landings. The large carrier, like the battleship, reached near perfection at the very time of its replacement as the most significant unit of the fleet, for the nuclear submarine, which was later to be armed with Polaris missiles, once more demonstrated the effect of developing technology.

HMS *Ark Royal* during air-training operations in the Central Mediterranean. In November 1970 the flight-deck was strengthened to allow operation of the 1,400 mph 'Phantom' all-weather strike aircraft, with air-to-air missiles and conventional nuclear bombs.

The main control panel of the *Dreadnought*, Britain's first nuclear-powered submarine.

The United States were first with this class of vessel and were generous in imparting much essential technical knowledge to Britain. By 1960 progress had made possible the launching of the submarine *Dreadnought* – as revolutionary in design as her battleship predecessor of 1906. Recalling Fisher's realization of the potential of the submarine, the new ship would doubtless have appealed to him. The *Dreadnought*, the eleventh of her name in the annals of the Navy, has a surface displacement of 3,500 tons. She is powered by a pressurized water-cooled reactor, to give her an underwater speed in excess of 20 knots, and she is manned by a crew of eighty-eight. Her principal role is to hunt and destroy enemy submarines. She and her later sister-ships are classed as fleet submarines. The Polaris ships are larger and are armed with sixteen missiles. They displace 7,500 tons when surfaced, are capable of high submerged speed and have great manœuvrability. Their names, *Renown*, *Repulse*, *Resolution* and *Revenge*, recall those of well-known capital ships of the past, the *Revenge* having been Drake's flagship during the Armada campaign and the *Renown* being the last battle-cruiser afloat.

Other new types include 'guided missile armed destroyers', a clumsy name for valuable ships. Modern frigates bear little resemblance to those which fought in the Battle of the Atlantic, and there are a large number of coastal and inshore minesweepers which belie their categories in having ocean-going characteristics and a considerable endurance. The work of sea survey, which has continued unbroken since the era of James Cook and which is regarded as setting a standard to the world, is aided today by the ubiquitous helicopter.

The Naval Departments first established in Tudor times survived until reforms which took place in 1832, when a Board of Admiralty became responsible for all affairs concerned with the fleet and the Navy Office, which had been concerned with supply but not policy, disappeared. In 1964 the Ministry of Defence took charge of all three armed services, under a Secretary of State. It was at first proposed that the Navy's more immediate affairs should be looked after by a 'Navy Board of the Defence Council', but after considerable debate it was decided to retain the word 'Admiralty' in the new structure. The services are supervised by Admiralty, Army and Air Force Boards of the Defence Council. The old Admiralty buildings are no longer used for sea affairs, but the board-room, in which so many momentous decisions were reached in the past, has been retained with its fittings, including a wind-indicator, and its portraits, including a very Italianized version of Nelson.

The nuclear submarine *Resolution* on exercises in the Firth of Clyde, March 1970.

Under the terms set forth in the White Paper which announced this fundamental change, it was stated that the Queen had 'graciously

consented to assume the title of Lord High Admiral', following some of her predecessors who had exercised this office in person. 'She will fly the flag of the Lord High Admiral at sea and at naval establishments ashore on official occasions, with the Royal Standard', so the document explained. 'This will perpetuate the name of an Office which goes back six hundred years, and which would otherwise be lost following the abolition of the Lords Commissioners who at present exercise the Office.'

The Queen's act recalled an association of the reigning house with the Navy which is far from being symbolic. James II, when Duke of York, commanded fleets in battle, as did his cousin, Prince Rupert. William IV served under Rodney and was a brother officer with Nelson in the West Indies. George V was a professional naval officer and George VI was present at Jutland in the battleship *Collingwood*. The Duke of Edinburgh is the second of his title to have followed a sea career, including experience under Cunningham's command in the Mediterranean during the Second World War. His uncle, Lord Mountbatten, has had a naval career of great distinction, including a period as First Sea Lord, a post which was held by his father, Prince Louis of Battenberg, at the beginning of the First World War. The tradition has been continued by the present Prince of Wales.

As we have seen, the broad aims of the British Navy may be reduced – at the risk of over-simplification – to the principles of challenge and maintenance. The challenge taken up by such men as Drake and Ralegh was that of Spain, which once claimed exclusive dominion over huge undeveloped areas of the globe. Successors under the Commonwealth and the later Stuarts struggled for predominance in the carrying trade, once unquestionably Dutch. Later still, the efforts of France to extend her territory not only in Europe but overseas were, so far as possible, contained. Once Britain had herself acquired an empire, the exercise of sea power became more necessary than ever.

After the end of the Napoleonic war, what had been won had to be sustained. The task occupied the whole of the nineteenth century and much of the twentieth. Today, the world situation has altered so radically that the task of the Navy appears straightforward – sharing the defence of the home islands and the trade of the country, protecting the few outposts overseas which are still the nation's direct responsibility and playing an important part in the complex alliances necessary to the balance of world power. Yet it remains exacting, demanding both continued vigilance and swift adaption to change or crisis. The size of the Navy, some eighty-three thousand officers and men, is smaller than it has ever been, though cost rises with the need for increasingly complex equipment.

The sailor of today is a very different man from his predecessors – freer, more knowledgeable, more inclined to question. Yet he belongs by descent to those who served under Cunningham, Beatty,

Jellicoe, Fisher, St Vincent, Nelson, Howe, Hawke, Anson, Blake and the Elizabethans, and sinister signs of deterioration are not apparent when he is called upon to act.

Samuel Pepys, who was the first of many civil servants able to identify himself completely with the sea profession, codified what he thought should be the attitude of those with the fleet. His biographer, Sir Arthur Bryant, sums up:

> To obey orders punctually and without question; and to hold the Regulations of the Admiralty as more sacred than the Ten Commandments; to do one's duty for one's bare wages without cavil and in the face of death; and to lay one's all in the keeping of the Navy in the belief that somehow in this world or some other the Service would care for and vindicate its own; such was the creed which the little scribe in the great wig taught the fighting men of the Stuart Navy.

The little scribe in the great wig has long been gathered to his fathers. An Admiralty that he would have recognized has ceased to exist. Wages are not so meagre as once they were, since a service as technically trained and equipped as the modern Navy has to compete with the rewards offered by other spheres of work. Yet the passage still has relevance, even in a nuclear age.

For in final analysis, whatever motive may lead a man or woman to join the Navy, once they become part of it, their problems are in one sense resolved. They are dedicated people, dedicated to the defence of their country, and to those obligations and duties which fall to the Navy as the result of national policy.

In earlier times, for officers, the motive was often enough the hope of prize-money and advancement: for the men it was all too often enlistment by force. Today it is a matter of choice, and as the service affords great opportunities, particularly in specialized training and in the chance for responsibility, it will continue to attract at least some proportion of the best of the country's youth. Every indication suggests that the 'best' is as good as ever and that opportunities will be as varied as in the past.

With the swiftly growing exploitation of the oceans and seas in all their aspects, it is certain that the need for a well-equipped, though no longer predominating, Navy remains strong. Through its submarines, specifically designed for the purpose, it will play its part in deterrence; and vessels of every type are likely to find themselves involved in local crises and in rescue operations, large and small.

Wherever they sail, the ships of the Navy continue to represent the nation. This has never been an unworthy role, and in spite of the prophets of gloom and a depressed economic climate, there is no reason why it ever should be.

SUGGESTIONS FOR FURTHER READING

LIST OF ILLUSTRATIONS

INDEX

SUGGESTIONS FOR FURTHER READING

BIBLIOGRAPHY

Albion, R. G. *Naval and Maritime History. An Annotated Bibliography*, 4th ed., revised, Mystic, Conn. 1972 and Newton Abbot 1973 (a useful work, far from inclusive, which lists books relating to the British as well as to other navies)

Higham, R. (ed.) *A Guide to the Sources of British Military History*, Berkeley and Los Angeles, California 1971 (includes chapters on Naval History)

GENERAL WORKS

Graham, G. S. *Empire of the North Atlantic*, London 1951

Hodges, H. W. and Hughes, E. A. (eds.) *Select Naval Documents*, Cambridge 1922

Hough, G. *Fighting Ships*, London 1969

Howarth, D. *Sovereign of the Seas*, London 1974

Kemp, P. (ed.) *History of the Royal Navy*, London 1969

Lewis, M. A. *The History of the British Navy*, Harmondsworth 1957

Lewis, M. A. *The Navy of Britain*, London 1948

Lloyd, C. C. *The Nation and the Navy*, London 1954

Lloyd, C. C. *The British Seaman*, London 1968

Mahan, A. T. *The Influence of Sea Power upon History, 1660–1783*, London 1892

Mathew, D. *The Naval Heritage*, London 1944

Richmond, H. W. *Statesmen and Sea Power*, London 1946

Robinson, C. N. *The British Tar in Fact and Fiction*, London 1909

Roskill, S. W. *The Strategy of Sea Power*, London 1962

Schofield, B. B. *British Sea Power*, London 1967

Warner, O. *The Navy*, Harmondsworth 1968

FOUNDATIONS

Corbett, J. C. *Drake and the Tudor Navy*, London 1912

Hadow, G. E. (ed.) *Sir Walter Ralegh. Selections*, Oxford 1917

Hampden, J. (ed.) *Francis Drake, Privateer*, London 1972

Lacey, R. *Sir Walter Ralegh*, London 1973

Lewis, M. A. *The Hawkins Dynasty*, London 1969

Marcus, G.S. *A Naval History of England. The Formative Centuries*, London 1961

Mattingley, G.M. *The Defeat of the Spanish Armada*, London 1959

Penn, C.D. *The Navy under the Early Stuarts*, London 1920

Quinn, D.B. (ed.) *The Hakluyt Handbook* (2 vols.), London 1974

Rowse, A.L. *The Expansion of Elizabethan England*, London 1955

Williamson, J.A. *The Age of Drake*, London 1938

Williamson, J.A. *Sir Francis Drake*, London 1952

WAR WITH THE DUTCH

Anderson, R.C. (ed.) *Journals and Narratives of the Third Dutch War*, London 1948

Boxer, C.R. (ed.) *Journal of Maarten H. Tromp* (2 vols.), Cambridge 1930

Bryant, A. *Samuel Pepys* (3 vols.), London 1933–38

Haley, K.H.D. *The Dutch in the Seventeenth Century*, London 1972

Ollard, R. *Man of War: Sir Robert Holmes and the Restoration Navy*, London 1969

Ollard, R. *Pepys*, London 1974

Oppenheim, M. *Administration of the Royal Navy to 1660*, London 1896

Powell, J.R. *Robert Blake: General-at-Sea*, London 1972

Rogers, P.G. *The Dutch in the Medway*, London 1970

Tedder, A.W. *The Navy of the Restoration: From the Death of Cromwell to the Peace of Breda*, Cambridge 1916

THE KING OVER THE WATER

Baugh, D.A. *British Naval Administration in the Age of Walpole*, Princeton 1965

Ehrman, J. *The Navy in the War of William III, 1689–1697*, Cambridge 1953

Hartman, C.H. *The Angry Admiral: Edward Vernon*, London 1953

Heaps, L. (ed.) *The Log of the Centurion*, London 1973

Merriman, R.D. (ed.) *Queen Anne's Navy*, London 1959

Owen, J.H. *War At Sea Under Queen Anne*, London 1938

Powley, E.B. *The English Navy and the Revolution of 1688*, London 1928

Williams, G. (ed.) *Documents Relating to Anson's Voyage Round the World, 1740–1744*, London 1967

THE SEVEN YEARS WAR

Beaglehole, J.C. (ed.) *The Journals of Captain James Cook, 1768–1780* (4 vols.), Cambridge 1955–1974 (vol. 3 is in two parts and vol. 4 contains the definitive biography)

Corbett, J.S. *England in the Seven Years War* (2 vols.), 2nd ed. London 1918

Furneaux, R. *The Seven Years War*, London 1973

Mackay, R.F. *Admiral Hawke*, Oxford 1965

Marcus, G. *Quiberon Bay*, London 1960

Pack, S.W.G. *Admiral Lord Anson*, London 1960

Stacey, C.P. *Quebec: The Siege and the Battle*, Toronto 1959

Syrett, D. (ed.) *The Siege and Capture of Havana, 1762*, London 1970

THE NAVY IN ADVERSITY

Creswell, J. *British Admirals of the Eighteenth Century: Tactics in Battle*, London 1972

James, W.R. *The British Navy in Adversity*, London 1926

Mackesy, P. *The War for America, 1775–1783*, London 1964

Mahan, A.T. *Major Operations in the War of American Independence*, London 1913

McGuffie, T.H. *The Great Siege of Gibraltar*, London 1965

Patterson, A.T. *The Other Armada*, London 1960

Richmond, H.W. *The Navy in India, 1763–1783*, London 1931

Spinney, D. *Rodney*, London 1969

THE LONG STRUGGLE WITH FRANCE

Bennett, G. *Nelson the Commander*, London 1972

Corbett, J.C. *The Campaign of Trafalgar*, London 1910

Dugan, J. *The Great Mutiny*, London 1966

Lewis, M.A. *A Social History of the Navy, 1793–1815*, London 1960

Lloyd, C.C. *St. Vincent and Camperdown*, London 1963

Marcus, G.L. *A Naval History of England: The Age of Nelson*, London 1971

Masefield, J. *Sea Life in Nelson's Time*, London 1905

Nicolas, N.H. *The Dispatches and Letters of Vice-Admiral Lord Viscount Nelson* (7 vols.), London 1844–46

Oman, C. *Nelson*, London 1947

Ryan, A.N. (ed.) *The Saumarez Papers: The Baltic 1808–1812*, London 1968

Warner, O. *The Glorious First of June*, London 1961

Warner, O. *The Life and Letters of Vice-Admiral Lord Collingwood*, London 1968

Warner, O. *Nelson*, London 1975

Warner, O. *Nelson's Battles*, 2nd ed. Newton Abbot 1971

MANY INVENTIONS

Brock, P.W. and Greenhill, B. *Steam and Sail in Britain and North America*, Newton Abbot 1973

Jameson, W.S. *The Most Formidable Thing: The Story of the Submarine from its Earliest Days to the End of World War 1*, London 1965

Lewis, M.A. *The Navy in Transition: A Social History 1814–1864*, London 1965

Lipscomb, F.W. *The British Submarine*, London 1954

Mackay, R. *Fisher of Kilverstone*, Oxford 1973

Manning, T.D. *British Destroyers*, London 1961

March, E. *British Destroyers*, London 1966

Marder, A. *British Naval Policy, 1880–1905*, London 1941

Padfield, P. *The Great Naval Race*, London 1974

Parkes, O. *British Battleships*, London 1958

Robertson, F.L. *The Evolution of Naval Armament*, 2nd ed. London 1968

Rowland, K.T. *Steam at Sea*, Newton Abbot 1970

THE FIRST WORLD WAR

Bennett, G. *Naval Battles of the First World War*, London 1968

Bennett, G. *Cowan's War. British Naval Operations in the Baltic, 1918–1920*, London 1964

Bush, E. *Gallipoli*, London 1975

Chalmers, W.S. *The Life and Letters of David, Earl Beatty*, London 1951

Churchill, W.S. *The World Crisis* (4 vols.), London 1923–27

Corbett, J.S. and Newbolt, H. *Naval Operations* (5 vols.), London 1920–31

Halpern, P.G. (ed.) *The Keyes Papers (1914–1918)*, London 1975

James, R.R. *Gallipoli*, London 1965
Jellicoe, Viscount *The Grand Fleet, 1914–1916*, London 1919
Marder, A. *From the Dardanelles to Oran*, London 1974
Marder, A. *From the Dreadnought to Scapa Flow* (5 vols.), London 1961–70
Patterson, A.T. *Jellicoe*, London 1969
Pollen, A. *The Navy in Battle*, London 1918
Roskill, W.S. *Naval Policy Between the Wars*, London 1968

THE ULTIMATE TRIAL: THE SECOND WORLD WAR

Chalmers, W.S. *Max Horton and the Western Approaches*, London 1950
Chalmers, W.S. *Full Cycle: The Biography of Admiral Sir Bertram Ramsey*, London 1959
Churchill, W.S. *The Second World War* (6 vols.), London 1948–53
Cunningham, Viscount *A Sailor's Odyssey*, London 1951
Grenfell, R. *The Bismarck Episode*, London 1948
Kemp, P.K. *Victory at Sea 1939–1945*, London 1957
Macintyre, D. *The Battle of the Atlantic*, London 1961
McLachlan, D. *Room 39, Naval Intelligence in Action, 1939–1945*, London 1968
Morison, S.E. *The Two Ocean War*, Boston 1963
Pack, S.W.C. *Cunningham the Commander*, London 1974
Roskill, S.W. *The War at Sea* (3 vols.), London 1954–61
Roskill, S.W. *The Navy at War, 1939–1945*, London 1960
Schofield, B.B., *The Russian Convoys*, London 1964
Vian, P. *Action This Day: a War Memoir*, London 1960

LATER EVENTS

Blackman, R.V.B. (ed.) *Jane's Fighting Ships*, London 1972 (this, the monumental 75th edition, includes succinct accounts of items in the modern fleet. There is as yet no authoritative history of the last thirty years of naval developments)
Hampshire, A. Cecil *The Royal Navy Since 1945*, London 1975
Ritchie, G.S. *The Admiralty Chart*, London 1967

LIST OF ILLUSTRATIONS

Frontispiece: *Resolution*; painting by Willem van de Velde the Younger, 1667. *National Maritime Museum, Greenwich*.

8 Late-medieval copy of a page from the fifth-century *Notitia Dignitatum*, showing the forts of the Count of the Saxon Shore. *Bodleian Library, Oxford*.

10 Seals of Hythe (twelfth–thirteenth century), Hastings (thirteenth century) and Rye (fifteenth century). *Archives Nationales, Paris. Photo Giraudon*.

Bayeux Tapestry; detail. *Episcopal Museum, Bayeux. Photo Giraudon*.

11 The Shipman; miniature added to the margin of the Ellesmere Manuscript of the *Canterbury Tales* (1400–10). *Henry E. Huntington Library, San Marino, California*.

12–13 Battle of Sluys, 1340; Italian illustration to a fourteenth-century French manuscript. *British Library, London*.

15 Gold noble of Edward III, 1360–69. *British Museum, London*.

16 *Henri Grâce à Dieu*; illustration from Anthony Anthony's roll, 1546. *Pepysian Library, Magdalene College, Cambridge. Courtesy of the Master and Fellows of Magdalene College. Photo Science Museum*.

17 Iron gun from the *Mary Rose*; drawing made in 1929. *Photo Science Museum*.

Mary Rose; illustration from Anthony Anthony's roll, 1546. *Pepysian Library, Magdalene College, Cambridge. Courtesy of the Master and Fellows of Magdalene College. Photo Edward Leigh*.

18–19 The 'Cowdray' print, showing the English encampment at Portsmouth and the beginning of the action between the French and English fleets, 19 July 1545. *Southsea Castle, Portsmouth*.

20 Detail of a medal of Elizabeth I, struck after the defeat of the Armada in 1588; designed by Nicholas Hilliard. *British Museum, London*.

21 The Spanish Armada and the English fleet in the Channel, with fire-ships going into Calais harbour, 1588; engraving by Rytter, *A Discourse Concerninge the Spanish Fleete*, London 1590. *British Library, London*.

22 The *Ark Royal*, flagship of Lord Howard of Effingham at the time of the Armada; anonymous English wood-cut, late sixteenth century. *British Museum, London*.

Sir Francis Drake; miniature by Nicholas Hilliard, 1581. *National Maritime Museum, Greenwich*.

23 Sir Walter Ralegh; miniature by Nicholas Hilliard, c. 1585. *The Viscount Morpeth*.

Lord Howard of Effingham; miniature by Nicholas Hilliard, 1605. *National Maritime Museum, Greenwich*.

24 Mariner's astrolabe, c. 1588. *National Maritime Museum, Greenwich*.

25 Sir Richard Grenville; painting by an anonymous artist, 1571. *National Maritime Museum, Greenwich*.

26 Peter Pett and the *Sovereign of the Seas*, built 1637; painting by Sir Peter Lely, c. 1645. *National Maritime Museum, Greenwich*.

27 Robert Rich, Earl of Warwick; painting by Daniel Mytens. *National Maritime Museum, Greenwich*.

28 Admiral Robert Blake; miniature by Samuel Cooper. *National Maritime Museum, Greenwich*.

Prince Rupert; stoneware bust by Dwight of Fulham, c. 1680. *British Museum, London*.

30 Action off Portland, 18–20 February 1653; engraving by Melchior Küsell *National Maritime Museum, Greenwich*.

31 Action off Leghorn, 12 March 1653; painting by Reinier Nooms, called Zeeman (c. 1623–before 1668). *Rijksmuseum, Amsterdam*.

32 General George Monck; miniature by Samuel Cooper, c. 1670. *By gracious permission of HM The Queen*.

33 Action off the Gabbard, 2–4 June 1653; etching by C. Jannson. *National Maritime Museum, Greenwich*.

Battle of Scheveningen, 1 July 1653; grisaille by Willem van de Velde the Elder, 1655. *National Maritime Museum, Greenwich*.

36 James, Duke of York, as Lord High Admiral; painting by Henri Gascar, 1672–73. *National Maritime Museum, Greenwich.*

38 'Four Days' Battle', 1–4 June 1666; engraving by J. Ottens. *National Maritime Museum, Greenwich.*

39 Surrender of the *Royal Prince* during the 'Four Days' Battle', 1–4 June 1666; engraving by W. Nieuwhoff from a design by Willem van de Velde the Younger. *National Maritime Museum, Greenwich.*

Burning of the *Royal Charles* during the 'Four Days' Battle', 1–4 June 1666; painting by an anonymous artist. *National Maritime Museum, Greenwich.*

40 Vice-Admiral Sir Christopher Myngs; painting by Sir Peter Lely, 1666. *National Maritime Museum, Greenwich.*

41 Escutcheon from the *Royal Charles. Rijksmuseum, Amsterdam.*

42 Edward Montague, Earl of Sandwich; painting by Sir Peter Lely, 1666. *National Maritime Museum, Greenwich.*

43 Burning of the *Royal James* during the Battle of Sole Bay, 28 May 1672; painting by P. Monamy. *National Maritime Museum, Greenwich.*

44 Table showing the 'General State of Account' of the Exchequer grant to the Treasurer of the Navy. From Samuel Pepys, *Memoires Relating to the State of the Royal Navy, 1690. British Museum, London.*

45 Samuel Pepys; painting after Sir Peter Lely, also attributed to John Greenhill, *c.* 1670. *Pepysian Library, Magdalene College, Cambridge. Courtesy of the Master and Fellows of Magdalene College. Photo Edward Leigh.*

46–47 Fire-ships among the fleet at the Battle of the Texel, 1673; painting attributed to Willem van de Velde the Elder. *National Maritime Museum, Greenwich.*

48 Greenwich Observatory from Croom Hill; painting by an anonymous artist, *c.* 1680. *National Maritime Museum, Greenwich.*

50–51 Beachy Head, 30 June 1690; engraving made by order of the Earl of Torrington, 1710. *National Maritime Museum, Greenwich.*

52 Action off Barfleur, 19 May 1692; grisaille by A. Salm. *National Maritime Museum, Greenwich.*

53 The destruction of the *Soleil Royal* at La Hogue, 23 May 1692; painting by P. Monamy. *National Maritime Museum, Greenwich.*

54 Royal Hospital, Greenwich; engraving from *Britannia Illustrata*, Vol. II, 1720, pl. 39.

55 Thomas Phillip's section of a first rate ship, *c.* 1700. *National Maritime Museum, Greenwich.*

56 Vigo, from the English side; 12 October 1702; drawing by Willem van de Velde the Younger. *National Maritime Museum, Greenwich.*

57 Admiral Sir George Rooke; painting by Michael Dahl. *National Maritime Museum, Greenwich.*

Plan of Gibraltar, 23 July 1704; coloured engraving by C. Allard. *National Maritime Museum, Greenwich.*

58 Admiral Sir John Leake; painting by Sir Godfrey Kneller. *National Maritime Museum, Greenwich.*

59 Plan of Port Mahon, Minorca, 1708; engraving by J. Basire. *National Maritime Museum, Greenwich.*

60 The taking of Porto Bello, Panama, 21 November 1739; painting by Samuel Scott. *National Maritime Museum, Greenwich.*

61 Admiral Edward Vernon; painting by Francis Hayman. *National Maritime Museum, Greenwich.*

62 'In Irons for getting drunk'; etching by Lieutenant Sheringham, published by George Cruikshank. *National Maritime Museum, Greenwich.*

63 Admiral Lord Anson; mezzotint by J. McArdell, 1755, after Sir Joshua Reynolds. *National Maritime Museum, Greenwich.*

64 'A Geometrical Plan and North-East Elevation of His Majesty's Dockyard at Deptford with Part of the Town'; engraving by P.C. Canot, 1753, after a design by T. Milton. *National Maritime Museum, Greenwich.*

65 Toulon, 11 February 1744; fourth of a set of six engravings by F. Selma. *National Maritime Museum, Greenwich.*

68–69 'Vue de la Ville de Louisbourg prise en dedans du Port. 1731'; watercolour by an anonymous artist. *Public Archives of Canada.*

69 Admiral John Byng; painting by T. Hudson, 1749. *National Maritime Museum, Greenwich.*

70 'The Shooting of Admiral Byng, on board the *Monarque*, March 14, 1757'; printed for 'Thomas Bowles, in St Paul's Church-Yard, and John Bowles & Son, at the Black-Horse, Cornhill'. *National Maritime Museum, Greenwich.*

71 Cutting out of the *Prudent* and *Bienfaisant*, Louisbourg, 26 July 1758; engraving by P.C. Canot, 1771, after a design by Paton. *National Maritime Museum, Greenwich.*

72 Battle of the Plains of Abraham, 13 September 1759; engraving by P.C. Canot, 1760, after a design by Captain Hervey Smyth. *National Maritime Museum, Greenwich.*

73 Midship section of a man-of-war; from William Falconer's *Universal Dictionary of the Marine*, 1769. *British Library, London.*

75 The *Warspite* at Lagos, 1759; pen and wash drawing. *National Maritime Museum, Greenwich.*

Admiral Lord Hawke; painting by Francis Cotes. *National Maritime Museum, Greenwich.*

Quiberon Bay, 1759; painting by R. Paton. *National Maritime Museum, Greenwich.*

78 Captain James Cook; painting by John Webber. *National Art Gallery, Wellington, New Zealand. Photo John Ashton.*

79 Captain Cook landing at Tanna, one of the New Hebrides, during his voyage of 1772–75; illustration from G.G. Anderson, *A New Atlantic.*

'A White Bear'; engraving by Mazell after J. Webber, from Cook's *Voyage to the Pacific*, 1784.

82 Richard Howe, 1st Earl; wax relief by John Flaxman. *National Portrait Gallery, London.*

83 Rear-Admiral Richard Kempenfelt; painting by Ralph Earl, 1783. *National Maritime Museum, Greenwich.*

84 *Romulus* taken by a French division in Chesapeake Bay, February 1781; coloured engraving. *National Maritime Museum, Greenwich.*

85 The relief of Gibraltar, 1781; painting by Dominic Serres. *Royal Academy of Arts, London.*

86 The sinking of the *Royal George* at Spithead, 29 August 1782; engraving. *Guildhall, Portsmouth.*

87 Prince William Henry on board the *Royal George*, under instruction in navigation by Admiral Digby; illustration from Hervey's *The Naval History.*

88 Admiral Lord Rodney; painting by Sir Joshua Reynolds. *The Royal Collection, St James's Palace. By gracious permission of HM The Queen.*

89 The surrender of St Eustacius to Rodney, 3 April 1781; wash and colour drawing by an anonymous artist. *National Maritime Museum, Greenwich.*

Action off Dogger Bank, 5 August 1781; plan by an officer on the spot, published by Thomas Colley, 9 August 1781. *National Maritime Museum, Greenwich.*

90 Admiral Rodney breaking the line at the Battle of 'the Saints', 1782; engraving by J. Wells after Thomas Walker. *National Maritime Museum, Greenwich.*

94 The *Queen Charlotte* at the Spithead review, 1790; painting attributed to W. Anderson. *National Maritime Museum, Greenwich.*

95 Duel between the *Crescent* and *Réunion*, 20 October 1793; one of a pair of aquatints engraved by J. W. Edy after Elliott, 1794. *National Maritime Museum, Greenwich.*

96 Portraits of the victors of the 'Glorious First of June', 1794; commemorative plate by R. Smirke, 1802. *National Maritime Museum, Greenwich.*

97 Lord Howe on the quarterdeck of the *Queen Charlotte*, 1 June 1794; painting by M. Brown. *National Maritime Museum, Greenwich.*

98 Admiral Lord Hood (1724–1816); painting by L. F. Abbott. *National Portrait Gallery, London.*

100 The Battle of Cape St Vincent, 14 February 1797; painting by W. Allan. *National Maritime Museum, Greenwich.*

101 Admiral Sir John Jervis, Earl of St Vincent; painting by Sir William Beechey. *National Maritime Museum, Greenwich.*

Nelson receiving the surrender of a Spanish ship, Cape St Vincent; painting by D. Orme. *National Maritime Museum, Greenwich.*

102 'A Seaman'; coloured aquatint by D. Serres, 1777. *National Maritime Museum, Greenwich.*

'A Master and Commander'; coloured aquatint by D. Serres, 1777. *National Maritime Museum, Greenwich.*

103 'The Point of Honour', a flogging at the gratings; engraving by George Cruikshank, 1825. *British Museum, London.*

104 'The Liberty of the Subject'; engraving by James Gillray, 1779. *Photo Courtauld Institute.*

105 'The Delegates in Council', the Nore Mutiny, 29 May 1797; engraving by George Cruikshank, 9 June 1797. *National Maritime Museum, Greenwich.*

106 Nelson on the quarterdeck of the *Vanguard*; painting by D. Orme. *National Maritime Museum, Greenwich.*

107 The Battle of the Nile; painting by Nicholas Pocock. *National Maritime Museum, Greenwich.*

108–09 The Battle of Copenhagen; painting by Nicholas Pocock. *National Maritime Museum, Greenwich.*

111 The *Victory* returning from Trafalgar; painting by J. M. W. Turner (1775–1851). *Collection of Mr and Mrs Paul Mellon.*

112 The *Arrow* and the *Acheron* attacked and taken by French frigates, 3–4 February 1805; engraving by F. Sartorius after J. Jeakes, 1805. *National Maritime Museum, Greenwich.*

113 'A Correct Plan and Elevation of the Famous French Raft'; engraving published by S. W. Fores, 1 February 1798. *British Museum, London.*

114 Sir Edward Codrington on the forecastle of the *Orion* at Trafalgar; painting by H. Wyllie. *Victory Museum, Portsmouth.*

115 The *Victory* towed into Gibraltar; engraving after Clarkson Stanfield. *National Maritime Museum, Greenwich.*

116 Popham captures the Cape of Good Hope from the Dutch, 4–10 January 1806; engraving by J. Clark and J. Hamble after W. M. Craig, 1806. *National Maritime Museum, Greenwich.*

117 Admiral Lord Collingwood; engraving by S. Cousins after a painting by Henry Howard. *National Maritime Museum, Greenwich.*

James Saumarez, Lord de Saumarez; mezzotint engraved by H. T. Ryall after S. Lane. *National Maritime Museum, Greenwich.*

118 The boarding of the *Chesapeake* by the officers and crew of the *Shannon*, 1 June 1813; aquatint engraved by Dubourg after Heath, 1816. *National Maritime Museum, Greenwich.*

119 The landing at Rangoon, Burma, 11 May 1824; one of a set of fifteen aquatints engraved by G. Hunt after J. Moore, 1825. *National Maritime Museum, Greenwich.*

The Battle of Navarino, 20 October 1827; engraving by W. Daniell, 1828. *National Maritime Museum, Greenwich.*

121 Midshipmen under instruction in navigation by the Master of a ship; painting by Nicholas Pocock. *National Maritime Museum, Greenwich.*

124 'Naval Eloquence', the Duke of Clarence as a rough sailor; engraving by James Gillray, 6 January 1795. *British Museum, London.*

125 Model of the *Charlotte Dundas*. *Photo Deutsches Museum, Munich.*

Pluto captures the slave barque *Orion*, 30 November 1859; lithograph by Taylor, 1876. *National Maritime Museum, Greenwich.*

126 Admiral Sir Charles Napier; painting by Thomas Joy. *National Maritime Museum, Greenwich.*

127 Mate Lucas wins the Victoria Cross, 21 June 1854; engraving by Day & Son after E. T. Dolby, 1854. *National Maritime Museum, Greenwich.*

128 Naval cutlass exercise; engraving by I. Girtin after Henry Angelo, Jr, with figures by J. Rowlandson, 1814. *National Maritime Museum, Greenwich.*

130 The *Merrimac* and the *Monitor* at Hampton Roads, 1862; lithograph. *National Maritime Museum, Greenwich.*

131 The *Captain*; coloured lithograph by T. G. Dutton, 1870. *National Maritime Museum, Greenwich.*

The *Devastation*. *National Maritime Museum, Greenwich.*

132 Royal Naval College, Dartmouth, 1910. *Imperial War Museum, London.*

133 The launch of the *Dreadnought*, 10 February 1906. *Imperial War Museum, London.*

134 The battle-cruiser *Invincible*. *Imperial War Museum, London.*

138 Sir Winston Churchill; oil sketch by Sir James Guthrie for his portrait in the group 'Statesmen of the Great War'. *Scottish National Portrait Gallery, Edinburgh. National Galleries of Scotland.*

Admiral Lord Fisher; painting by Augustus John. *Leicester Museums and Public Gallery.*

139 The battleship *Audacious* sinking, October 1914. *Imperial War Museum, London.*

140 Diagram of the Battle of Jutland, 31 May 1916. *Reproduced from the original by R. D. Crawford, by permission of the Encyclopaedia Britannica. Photo Imperial War Museum, London.*

141 The loss of the battle-cruiser *Queen Mary* at Jutland. *Imperial War Museum, London.*

142 The U.35 torpedoes a merchant ship in the Mediterranean, April 1917. *Imperial War Museum, London.*

143 British naval airship escorts a convoy during the First World War. *Imperial War Museum, London.*

145 Admiral Jellicoe; painting by R. G. Eves, 1935. *National Portrait Gallery, London.*

Admiral Beatty; painting by A. S. Cope. *National Maritime Museum, Greenwich.*

146 HMS *Furious* with her complement of Sopwith 'Camels'. *Imperial War Museum, London.*

148 German 'pocket battleship' *Admiral Scheer*. *Imperial War Museum, London.*

149 German U-boat bunker, Trondheim, Norway. *Imperial War Museum, London.*

153 The *Admiral Graf Spee* in flames, Montevideo, December 1939. *Imperial War Museum, London.*

154 Malta convoy from the air; German photograph released in Britain in 1945. *Imperial War Museum, London.*

155 The RAF assists in the evacuation of Greece. *Imperial War Museum, London.*

156 The *Bismarck* exercising in the Baltic; photograph taken from the *Prinz Eugen*. *Imperial War Museum, London.*

157 HMS *Hood*. *Imperial War Museum, London.*

158 A ship's boat assisted through the ice by a Russian naval tug. *Imperial War Museum, London.*

159 HMS *Prince of Wales* leaves Singa-pore, 8 December 1941. *Imperial War Museum, London.*

160 Dieppe: landing craft. *Imperial War Museum, London.*

161 HMS *Prince of Wales* meeting an Atlantic convoy. *Imperial War Museum, London.*

162 The *Scharnhorst* in the Arctic. *Imperial War Museum, London.*

163 HMS *Duke of York*. *Imperial War Museum, London.*

164–65 D-Day, June 1944: British troops landing with bicycles. *Imperial War Museum, London.*

166 The British fleet in action off Sumatra. *Imperial War Museum, London.*

167 HMS *Formidable* hit by a Japanese suicide plane. *Imperial War Museum, London.*

168 British merchant convoy during the Second World War. *Imperial War Museum, London.*

170 The *Amethyst* reaches Hong Kong, 8 August 1949. *Photo Associated Press.*

171 HMS *Ocean* on her way to Korea from Japan, 21 July 1952. *Imperial War Museum, London.*

172 Suez: casualties from a Royal Navy helicopter on board HMS *Eagle*, 11 November 1956. *Photo Associated Press.*

173 HMS *Ark Royal* during air-training operations in the Central Mediterranean: a 'Phantom' aircraft being positioned for take-off. *British Official Photograph. Central Office of Information.*

174 The main control panel of the nuclear submarine *Dreadnought*. *Photo Associated Press.*

175 The nuclear submarine *Resolution* in the Firth of Clyde near Helensburgh, March 1970. *British Official Photograph. Central Office of Information.*

INDEX

Page numbers in italic refer to illustrations

Academy, Royal Naval 120
Admiralty, Board of 66, 175, 176
Alfred the Great 9
Altmark, SS 152
Amiens, Treaty of 110
Anson, Admiral Lord 63, 67, 92; circumnavigation 62–64; administration 65; Finisterre, Battle of 65
Armada, Spanish 21
'Armed Neutrality' of the North 109
astrolabe 24
Athenia, SS 150, 152
aviation, naval 136, 143, 145, 146, 147, 151, 166, 170, 172, 173
Ayscue, Sir George 37

Ball, Sir Alexander 106
Baltic operations 145
Banks, Sir Joseph 77
Barfleur, Battle of 52
Barham, Lord 48, 83, 95
Beachy Head, Battle of 49, 50, 51
Beatty, Admiral of the Fleet, Earl 135, 144, 145; as Naval Secretary 135; commands battle-cruisers 135; at Heligoland 138; at Dogger Bank 139; at Jutland 139, 140; commands Grand Fleet 144; as First Sea Lord 144, 147
Bridport, Lord see Hood, Alexander
Brigandyn, Robert 14
Broke, Sir Philip 118
Bryant, Sir Arthur 176
Burnett, Admiral 164
Byng, Admiral 67–68, 69, 70

Calder, Sir Robert 113
Caldwell, Admiral 95
Camperdown, Battle of 105
Carew, Sir George 16
carronades 120
Chads, Commander James 72
Charles I 25, 26
Charles II 41, 42, 43
Charlotte Dundas, SS 124
Chaucer's 'Shipman' 10, 11
Chesapeake 84, 85, 92
Churchill, Sir Winston 132, 136, 138, 151, 152

Cinque Ports 9, 10, 11, 14, 48; seals of 10
Clarendon, Lord 34
Cochrane, Lord 124
Codrington, Sir Edward 96, 114, 118
Colbert, Jean-Baptiste 50
Coles, Captain Cowper 130
Collingwood, Admiral Lord 92, 104, 113, 114, 116, 117
Collins, Captain Greenville 47
Conrad, Joseph 115, 123
Cook, Captain James 72, 78, 79; circumnavigation 77–80
Copenhagen, attacks on 108, 109, 110
coppering of ships 87
Cornwallis, Sir William 92, 110, 113
Count of the Saxon Shore 8, 9
Cradock, Sir Christopher 138
Crete 155–57
Cromwell, Oliver 29, 34
Cunibert, Vittorio 133
Cunningham, Admiral of the Fleet, Viscount 145, 155, 156, 157, 161, 164
Curtis, Sir Roger 95, 96

Dardanelles 137, 151
Dartmouth, Royal Naval College 132
Deane, Richard 31
Deptford Dockyard 64
Dieppe 160
Dogger Bank, Battles of 88, 89, 139
Dönitz, Admiral 159
Douglas, Sir Charles 91
Drake, Sir Francis 21, 22
Dryden, John 44
Duff, Captain Robert 74
Duncan, Admiral 105
Dundas, Sir Richard 126
Dunkirk 153, 165

Edinburgh, Duke of 176
Edward III 12, 13, 15
Elizabeth I 19, 20
Elizabeth II 175, 176
Exmouth, Lord 118

Fighting Instructions 120
Fisher, Admiral of the Fleet, Lord 123, 138; as First Sea Lord 132; seamen

entry 132; ship construction 133; submarines 135; returns to Admiralty 137, 138
Fleet Air Arm see aviation, naval
'fleet in being', origin of 50
flogging 103, 104, 136
Foley, Captain 107
'Four Days' Battle', the 37, 38, 39
Fraser, Admiral of the Fleet, Sir Bruce 164, 166
Frederick the Great 70
Frobisher, Martin 23

Gabbard, Battle of the 32
Gardner, Admiral Lord 95
George II 70, 77
George III 77, 93
George V 176
George VI 176
Gibraltar: capture of 56, 57; relief 85, 86
'Glorious First of June', Battle of the 94, 96, 97
Good Hope, Cape of 116, 117
Grasse, Comte de 85, 90
Graves, Admiral 85, 95
Greenwich Hospital 54, 80
Greenwich Observatory 48
Grenville, Sir Richard 25
grog 61, 102
Guichen, Admiral de 87, 90
guns 120, 121, 129

Hakluyt, Richard 14, 25
Hamilton, Emma 109
Hamilton, Sir William 107
Hardy, Captain Thomas 104
Havana 74
Hawke, Admiral Lord 65, 71, 75; at Quiberon Bay 72, 74, 75, 76, 77
Hawkins, Sir John 23
Heathfield, Lord 85
Heligoland Bight, Battle of 138
Henry V 14
Henry VII 14
Henry VIII 15, 18
Herbert, Arthur, Earl of Torrington 49, 50
Hipper, Admiral von 139–41

Holland, John 135
Holmes, Sir Robert 41, 45
Hood, Alexander, later Lord Bridport 93, 95
Hood, Samuel, later Lord Hood 85, 88, 93, 97, 98
Horton, Admiral Sir Max 145, 161, 162
Hoste, Sir William 123, 129
Howard of Effingham, Lord 6, 21, 23
Howe, Earl 65, 82, 97, 108; at Rochefort 71; at Quiberon Bay 76; in America 81; relieves Gibraltar 86; as First Lord 93; 'Glorious First of June' 94–97; at Spithead Mutiny 104
Howe, Sir William 81
Hungerford, Lord 14

Indonesia 172

Jamaica 35, 90
James I 7, 23, 24
James II 35, 36, 37, 43, 45, 48, 49, 53, 176
Japan 133, 146, 159
Jellicoe, Admiral of the Fleet, Earl 139–41, 142, 144, 145
Jervis, John, later Earl of St Vincent 72, 99, 100
Johnson, Samuel 6, 55, 103
Jutland, Battle of 139, 140, 141, 142

Kempenfelt, Rear-Admiral Richard 83, 86
Kentish Knock, Battle of the 30
Keppel, Admiral, Viscount 65, 74, 82
Kerens, Lieutenant Commander 169, 170
Korea 170
Kuwait 172

Laubeuf, Maxime 135
Lawson, Sir John 81
Leake, Sir John 58
Leghorn, action off 31
Lestock, Admiral 66
'Libel of English Policy, The' 14
Lind, James 64, 91
Londonderry, relief of 49
Lord Admiral, office of 18, 66, 176
Louisbourg 67, 68–69, 71

Mahan, A.H. 94, 110, 133
Malta 107, 110, 154, 157, 165
Manila 74
Manning 121, 127
Marder, Professor Arthur 144
Marines, Royal 58, 72, 165, 170, 172
Marryat, Captain Frederick 118, 124
Masefield, John 122
Matapan, Battle of 155
Matthews, Admiral Thomas 65
Medina Sidonia, Duke of 20
Middleton, Charles see Barham, Lord
Minorca 59, 68
Moleyns, Adam de 14
Monck, George, Duke of Albemarle 31, 32, 35, 37
Montague, Admiral 97
Morgan, Charles 136
Mountbatten, Earl 160, 176
mutiny (1797) 99, 100, 104, 105
Myngs, Sir Christopher 40

Napier, Admiral Sir Charles 126
naval clubs 45
Navarino 118, 119
Navy Board 17, 45
Nelson, Vice-Admiral, Viscount 67, 92, 94, 106, 121, 123, 129; at Corsica 99; at St Vincent 100; pursues French 106; wins Battle of the Nile 107–09; at Copenhagen 109, 110; attacks Boulogne 110; watches Toulon 110; at Trafalgar 113–15
Nordenfelt, Torsten 135
Normandy, invasion of 165

Observatory, Royal 47, 48
officers, entry of into Navy 120

Palliser, Admiral Sir Hugh 77, 82
Parker, Sir Hyde (the Elder) 88
Parker, Sir Hyde (the Younger) 109, 110
Parker, Richard 105
Pasley, Admiral 95
pay, rate of 19, 35, 100, 104
Penn, William 34
Pepys, Samuel 40, 43, 44, 45, 48, 176, 177
Pett, Peter 26
Pett, Phineas 24
Philip II of Spain 20, 30
Pitt, William (the Elder) 70
Pocock, Sir George 74
Polaris submarines 173
Popham, Sir Home 117
Portland, action off 30
Porto Bello 60
Portsmouth, Battle of 18, 19
Pound, Sir Dudley 152, 161
PQ 17, convoy to Russia 158
press gang 48, 104, 127
Price, Rear-Admiral David 127
prize money 74

Quebec 71, 72, 73, 80, 117

Ralegh, Sir Walter 6, 21, 23, 24, 25
Ramsey, Sir Bertram 165
Richardson, William 122
Riel, Hervé 53
Rochefort 71, 76
Rodney, Admiral Lord 85, 87, 88; relieves Gibraltar 86; beats de Grasse 90, 91
Rooke, Sir George 53, 56
Rowley, Rear-Admiral Joshua 88
Rupert, Prince 27, 28, 37, 46, 176
Russell, Edward, Earl of Orford 49
Ruyter, Admiral de 37, 38, 41

St André, Jean-Bon 95
St Nazaire 160
St Vincent, Battle of 100
St Vincent, Lord see Jervis, John
Sandwich, Earl of 42, 43
Saumarez, Sir James 90, 92, 94, 106, 107, 116, 117
Saumarez, Captain Philip 65
Saunders, Sir Charles 65, 72
Scheer, Admiral 139, 140
Scheveningen, Battle of 33
Scott, Sir Percy 131
scurvy 64, 77, 91

ships (British): Aboukir 138; Acheron 112; Achilles 152; Adventure 77; Agamemnon 94; Ajax 152; Alexander 106; Amethyst 169, 170; Ark Royal 6, 22, 173; Arrow 112; Audacious 138; Barfleur 54, 90; Barham 134, 157; Britannia 132; Burford 61; Canada 92; Captain 100, 130, 131; Centurion 62; Cossack 152; Courageous 152; Crescent 94, 95; Cressy 138; Devastation 130, 131; Diana 118; Dreadnought 133, 134, 174; Duke of York 163, 164; Eagle 172, 173; Endeavour 77; Engadine 147; Essex 76; Exeter 152; Formidable 91, 167; Furious 146; Ganges 130; Goliath 106, 107; Golden Hind 21; Grâce Dieu 15, 16; Henri Grâce à Dieu 16; Hermes 147; Hogue 138; Hood 156, 157; Illustrious 132, 155; Indefatigable 140; Invincible 134, 141; Lion 139, 140; Magnanime 71, 76; Marlborough 132; Mary Rose 16, 17; Mutine 106; Nelson 146; Norfolk 156, 164; Ocean 171; Orion 106, 114; Pluto 125; Prince 24; Prince of Wales 156, 159; Queen Charlotte 93, 94, 96; Queen Elizabeth 134, 157; Queen Mary 140, 141; Regent 15; Renown 174; Repulse 159, 174; Resolution Frontispiece, 76, 174, 175; Revenge 25, 37, 174; Rodney 146; Romulus 84; Royal Charles 37, 41; Royal George 76, 86; Royal James 43; Royal Oak 152; Royal Prince 38; Russell 90; Shannon 118; Sovereign of the Seas 26; Suffolk 156; Swiftsure 37; Téméraire 124; Valiant 157; Vanguard 106, 164; Victory 103, 104, 110, 111, 115, 116, 120, 124; Warspite 75, 151, 165; Warrior 129; York 157
ships (French): Formidable 76; Gloire 129; L'Orient 108; Narval 135; Montagne 95; Océan 130; Redoubtable 115; Réunion 94, 95; Soleil Royal 52, 53, 76; Superbe 76; Thésée 76; Ville de Paris 90; Zélée 90
ships (German): Admiral Scheer 148; Bismarck 156; Blücher 139; Breslau 137; Goeben 137; Graf Spee 152, 153; Prinz Eugen 156; Scharnhorst 162, 164; Seydlitz 139; Tirpitz 158
ships (Spanish): Nuestra Señora de Covadonga 64; Santo Domingo 87
ships (United States): Chesapeake 118; Constitution 117; Merrimac 129, 130; Monitor 129, 130
Simpson, Rear-Admiral G. W. G. 136
slave trade, suppression of 125
Sluys, Battle of 12, 13
Smith, Sir Sydney 99, 108
Sole Bay, Battle of 43
Spee, Count von 138
Spragge, Sir Edward 47
Suffren, Bailli de 83, 84, 92
Surcouf, Robert 115, 116

tactics, naval 24, 120, 143, 146, 147
Taranto, raid on 155
Texel, Battle of the 46, 47
Togo, Admiral 133
torpedoes 130, 131, 135
Toulon 65

Tourville 52
Tromp, Marten 30, 31, *38*

U-boat warfare 140, 142, 143, *149*, 150,
  152, 159, 163
uniform, naval 102, 127, 129
United States 143, 147, '61, 169, 174

Venables, Robert 34, 35
Vernon, Admiral 59, 60, *61*, 62, 122
Vian, Sir Philip 152, 165
victualling 102, 121, 122
Vigo *56*

Villaret-Joyeuse, Admiral 96, 97
Villeneuve, Admiral 112, 113
Voltaire 70

Walker, Captain F.J. 163
Walker, Sir Walter 172
Wallis, Captain Samuel 77
Warner, Sir Thomas 84
Warwick, Earl of *27*
Washington Conference 145, 146
Washington, George 84
Webb, Sir Aston 132
Wellington, Duke of 115

Whitehead, Robert 130
William III 49, 58
William IV *87*, 124, *125*, 176
Wolfe, General James 71, 72, 73
Women's Royal Naval Service (WRNS)
  151

York, Duke of *see* James II
Yorke, James Sidney 91, 92

Zeebrugge, raid on 143
Zeppelin airships 136, 140, 147